Günter Ullrich/Michael McTear

The Student's Pocketbook of Technical English

Eine Einführung in die Grundlagen für Schule und Beruf

Ferdinand Schöningh
Paderborn · München · Wien · Zürich

Verlagsredaktion:

Ernest Pasakarnis
Gerald Williams

Illustrationen:

Gus
Horst Weckwert

München · Wien · Zürich
Printed in Germany
Herstellung: Ferdinand Schöningh, Paderborn

ISBN 3–506–40551–9

Inhaltsverzeichnis

Listen

Vorwort

Das vorliegende Taschenbuch ist aus der Arbeit mit Schulklassen der zweistufigen Berufsfachschule für Technik (BFT) entstanden und soll dem Berufsschullehrbuch "Nine to Five" als Parallelkurs für diese Fachklassen dienen.
Nach Anlage und Aufbau des Buches kann es auch mit jedem anderen Lehrbuch kombiniert werden, das Wortschatz und grammatische Strukturen vermittelt, die sich an einen Anfängerkurs anschließen. Als Einführung in den technischen Wortschatz wird es auch dem Fachoberschüler, Fachhochschulstudenten und dem Techniker, der sich erstmalig von Berufs wegen mit diesem englischen Wortschatz befassen muß, von Nutzen sein. Es wird ein Kenntnisstand vorausgesetzt, der als Grundlagenwissen auch dem Schüler verbleibt, der nach mehrjährigem Aussetzen von neuem mit der Arbeit in der englischen Sprache beginnt.
Eine weitere Verwendungsmöglichkeit sehen wir für die Arbeit mit den Klassen 9 und 10 der Hauptschulen, Realschulen und Gymnasien und für die Volkshochschulkurse. Die Verfasser wissen aus eigener Erfahrung, wie schwer es ist, für diese Altersstufe angemessenes Lektürematerial zu finden, welches das Interesse für einen etwas längeren Zeitraum zu fesseln vermag. Diese Schülergruppe wird die sprachlichen und grammatischen Anforderungen leichter bewältigen können und durch den umfangreichen und abwechslungsreichen technischen Wortschatz viel Anregung gewinnen.
Wir halten einen Elementarwortschatz von etwa 800–1000 Wörtern für erforderlich, darin enthalten die Kenntnis der wichtigsten unregelmäßigen Verben, der Fragebildung und Verneinung in den einfachen Zeiten, der vollständigen Hilfsverben, der Pluralbildung und der Steigerung der Adjektive. Diese Strukturen werden in den Übungen befestigt und erweitert. In den ersten Lektionen kommen Übungen zum Gebrauch der unvollständigen (modalen) Hilfsverben hinzu, von Lektion 5 ab die Arbeit mit dem Present Perfect und in der Lektion 14 die Anwendung von Passivkonstruktionen.

Wie die Lektionen, die mit Situationsdialogen und Informationstexten in Stil und Formulierung mit sorgfältiger Auswahl von Redewendungen gesprochenes Umgangsenglisch bieten, dienen auch die Übungstexte der Förderung der Sprech- und Dialogfähigkeit.
Bei der Erprobung einzelner Lektionen ergab sich, daß man etwa ein Schuljahr für das Taschenbuch benötigen wird, wenn man es mit einer Wochenstunde zusätzlich zum Hauptlehrbuch und anderem Unterrichtsmaterial einsetzt. Es sei noch einmal vermerkt, daß es kein eigenständiges Lehrbuch ist. Wer im Selbststudium arbeitet oder in einem Fremdsprachenkurs, der von einem Unternehmen eingerichtet wurde, sollte ein einfaches Wörterbuch und einen kurzen Abriß der Elementargrammatik mit benutzen.
Die im Anhang angebotenen Listen sollen dem interessierten Schüler und Techniker eine erste Orientierung im Bereich einiger technischer Wortfelder geben. Sie sind, wie das ganze Taschenbuch, als eine Einführung gedacht und damit auch als Vorstufe zur Arbeit mit weiterführenden Fachbüchern für technisches Englisch an Kollegstufen und Hochschulen bestimmt.
Bei der Gestaltung der einzelnen Lektionen und der Auswahl des Wortschatzes gaben uns die Mitarbeiter der neusprachlichen Abteilung des Verlages und die Werkstattlehrer der Kreisberufsschule in Lünen, Herr Ing. Loddoch und Herr Ing. Becker, viele wertvolle Hilfen und Anregungen, für die wir an dieser Stelle herzlichen Dank sagen.

Günter Ullrich
Lünen

Michael McTear
Belfast

Lesson 1A

Do It Yourself

Hallo, everybody! – Do you know how easy it is to be a do it yourself enthusiast?
Come and pay us a visit!
We are opening your new "Do It Yourself Centre" and offer you all the tools and material you need.
Do you want to paper your dining-room? – to tile your bathroom? – to make a bookcase? – a shelf?
Whatever it is, here is everything you want!
Boards and timber of different sizes, colours and types.
Choose one of our new electric saws.
Buy a set of screwdrivers, bits, chisels.
Don't forget a new rule!
Housewives, if your husbands are all thumbs and can't hammer a nail in straight, buy them one of our electric drills!
After a few days you will have a do it yourself worker who can do many small repair jobs in the house himself.

Lesson 1B

How to Make a Bookcase

The Harpers, Fred and his wife Jane, are sitting at the breakfast table. They are studying the newspaper, Fred the football results, Jane the adverts.

Jane: "Look at this Fred, this is very interesting".
Fred: "What? Another bargain at the boutique?"
Jane: "No, a leaflet in the paper from the d.i.y. centre. It's a set of instructions – How to make a bookcase"
Fred: "Let me see".

..... if our prefabricated pieces are too big or too small for your bookcase, tell us the measurements and we'll cut the wood to the right size.
Then you measure the joints with a rule and mark them with a pencil.
Cut them out with a chisel, join the pieces together and drill some holes in the wood to make the joints stronger.
Put screws in the holes and screw them in.
If you want to paint your bookcase, don't forget – three coats:
Primer, undercoat, top coat
"Well, that seems to be very easy. I think I'll make a new bookcase on Saturday afternoon".

Exercises 1:

a) Answer these questions:
   1. What do d.i.y. shops offer?
   2. What information does Jane find in the newspaper?
   3. What pages of the newspaper does Fred usually study?

4. What do housewives buy for their husbands?
5. What does Fred want to do in his free time on Saturday?

b) Fill in the right word:
chisel – screws – to measure – saw – nails – prefabricated – to drill – set of instructions.
1. You can make a shelf very quickly if you buy ..... pieces of timber.
2. You must read the ..... before you begin.
3. You cut the wood with a ..... and you cut out the joints with a .....
4. You ..... the holes and then you put in the .....
5. You ..... the size with a rule.
6. You must hammer the ..... in straight.

c) Read what the d.i.y. enthusiast does. Use the following verbs: to bring – to take – to fetch.
Example: He ..... the tools from the d.i.y. centre.
(He fetches the tools from the d.i.y. centre).
1. He ..... the wood to the electric saw to cut it to size.
2. His son ..... him the toolbox and he ..... out a hammer and some nails.
3. He ..... the rule to measure the joints.
4. His wife ..... him a bottle of beer to make the work quicker.

d) What happened on Saturday when Fred Harper made his bookcase?
Fill in the right verbs – past tense (to buy – to cut – to go – to take – to forget).
Example: He ..... the set of instructions.
(He read the set of instructions).
1. He ..... some pieces of wood.
2. He ..... them to size.
3. He ..... to the d.i.y. centre to fetch the paint.
4. He ..... the screwdriver.
5. He ..... to mark the joints with a pencil.

Lesson 2A

Good Advice from an Expert

Every evening when Fred Harper comes home from his office he can see his neighbour working at his bench in his little workshop.

His neighbour is a very skilful mechanic who does a lot of repairs in his free time.

When Fred went over one afternoon to ask him for a file, he was surprised to see such a lot of tools. His neighbour suggested that Fred should set up a workshop himself in the shed behind the house.

He gave him many useful hints and a list of tools for his basic equipment. When Fred looked at the list and thought of the prices, he knew that they would have to cut down on house-keeping money.

But on the other hand they would save money.

"Do it yourself and you don't have so many workman's bills to pay ", he said to himself.

Lesson 2B

Checking the List

Jane: "Now look, Fred, the list says – several hammers, pincers, screwdrivers, spanners – we've got all those tools in our toolbox already".

Fred: "That's right, dear, but we need a set of spanners and a set of screwdrivers. Think of Jim's bike and our lawn mower. Nearly every week we have to tighten or loosen nuts and bolts".

Jane: "All right, but what about these things? Wood screws, wing screws, wing nuts, rawl plugs, screws, spacers, bolts and nuts with different threads and heads, square, and – what's this – hexagonal? Can you get all these at the d.i.y. centre, too?"

Fred: "Well, I think the local hardware shop will have them. By the way, have we got a pair of pincers?"

Jane: "Yes, we have, but what I want is a pair of pliers to pull out nails and to cut wires when I'm working in the garden. Is there one on the list?"

Fred: "Of course, there is. Now – saws. Let me see – we have a handsaw, a fretsaw and an old framesaw, which is still good. We must buy a hacksaw. Do you remember, we had to ask Jack Turner for the hacksaw last summer to cut the old iron hinges to size for the new garden gate?"

Jane: "All right, the next item on the list – a set of bits for the electric drill – I bought them last week and a new gimlet. But Fred, two wrenches and a big vice, do you really need these tools?"

Fred: "Yes, I do. You can adjust a wrench and it fits even the big cap nuts and stop nuts. You know, sometimes a bolt or a lock nut won't come off and ....."

Jane: "Fred, are you a clerk or are you a plumber? Everybody knows that nuts, bolts and screws are your new hobby but if you can't talk about something else our friends will think that you're nuts or that you've got a screw loose".

Fred: "Now Jane, don't be a spoilsport. Just one more tool. A plane for my woodwork".

Exercises 2:

a) Here is a list of jobs and a list of tools. Find the right tool for the right job:

jobs	tools
1. we cut the wood to size with a	hammer
2. we cut out joints with a	screwdriver
3. we plane the wood with a	rule
4. we drive in nails with a	hacksaw
5. we drive in screws with a	drill
6. we tighten and loosen nuts with a	saw
7. we drill a hole for a rawl plug with a	spanner
8. we cut iron with a	plane
9. we loosen big stop nuts with a	chisel
10. we measure a piece of wood with a	wrench

b) Form questions. Ask for the words in italics:

Example: The *neighbour* gives Fred a *hacksaw* (who; what). (Who gives Fred a hacksaw? What does the neighbour give Fred?)

1. The *worker* buys a new *wrench.* (who; what)
2. He puts the *pliers* in the *toolbox*. (what; where)
3. *The mechanic* fetches a *set of spanners* (who; how many)
4. He keeps *the nuts* in *two boxes.* (what; where)

c) Translate into German:

1. Don't take this bolt; it's got the wrong thread.
2. You can't use this saw; take a hacksaw.
3. You mustn't leave the tools on the bench.
4. You needn't take a wrench; take a spanner.

d) Fill in: don't – needn't – can't – mustn't

1. ..... you see these marks on the wood?
2. No; I ..... see them.
3. You ..... use nails for this bookcase. It's better to use screws.
4. I bought a hacksaw last week, so we ..... ask the neighbour.

Lesson 3A

A Visit to the Factory

Fred Harper arrives home later than usual and his wife is waiting for him.

Fred: "Hallo, Jane, sorry I'm late. Jack Turner next door called at the office and asked me to take him home. There is something wrong with his car. He has taken it to the garage to check the engine."

Jane: "Did you have a look at the factory where he works?"

Fred: "Well, as a matter of fact, I wanted to have a look at all the machines, but he was in a hurry today. He promised to show me everything the day after tomorrow".

Jane: "What machine does he operate?"

Fred: "Well, he operates several machines, but he usually works at a lathe. – Isn't that funny? Jack's name is Turner and he operates a lathe".

Jane: "Yes, it is. Now I can only hope that you are not going to buy a harp because your name is Harper".

Fred: "Good idea! I must think it over! Anyway, the day after tomorrow I'll be late again. Jack and I will be home about seven o'clock".

Jane: "All right, dinner can wait. But you must promise me not to buy a machine at the factory. Our shed is full of tools already".

OPERATING MACHINES

Lesson 3B

Machines and Their Functions

Jack Turner: "Look, you put in a piece of material here and this here is the turning tool. I start the lathe and regulate the revolutions (revs.), that's the speed. Now the workpiece is rotating very fast and I can process it in different ways. What you learn first is straight turning (cylindrical turning) and facing. Then you try form turning, that is, you give the workpiece a profile. You see, with this turret lathe you can do a lot of operations".

Fred Harper: "Can you drill a hole into this round bar steel?"

Jack: "Of course I can. Look here, this is the boring tool".

Fred: "Yes, I see. May I try to turn the lathe off?"

Jack: "Nothing easier than that. Pull this switch here. Everybody can start or stop machines. You just press or push in a button, turn a knob, a switch or pull down or push up a lever. But take my word for it, it takes some time to become an experienced machinist".

Fred: "Yes, I can imagine that. We clerks only think of our office work and don't know much about your jobs".

Jack: "By the way, you've bought your planes at the d.i.y. center, haven't you? Now look at these machines. They are planes, too, but for metal and not for wood. We have two different types. This one is a planer and that one is for shaping, a shaper as we call it. There are special tools for shaping and planing and it is not easy for a beginner to understand all these different things and operations".

Fred: "And what kind of operations can you do with this milling machine? Can you cut grooves?"

Jack: "Of course I can, but what I usually do is slab-milling. Here is the spindle with the plain milling cutter. And the other machine is set for shell-end milling. With different metals you always have to fix the right milling cutter".

Fred: "And those big machines over there?"

Jack: "Oh, they are automatic presses and punching machines. It's a good thing that they are not working at the moment; you wouldn't like the noise".

Lesson 3C

Learn from an Experienced Machinist

1. Read the operating instructions.
2. Keep your eyes on the machine while it is working.
3. Check your machine at regular intervals.
4. Don't forget to grease and lubricate it.
5. Keep a set of spare parts handy to replace parts which are worn or broken.
6. Never try to disassemble and reassemble complicated machines. Leave that to a fitter.

Exercises 3:

a) Answer these questions (Past tense).
   1. When did Fred arrive home?
   2. Where did Jack Turner take his car?
   3. What did the machinist keep handy for his broken parts?
   4. Who did he leave the repair of the machine to?
   5. Where did Fred go after work to fetch his neighbour?
   6. What did he buy for his workshop?

b) Find the right words from the list to fill the gaps: (tool, lever, experienced, punching machines, spindle, turning tool, slab-milling, spare parts, turret lathe, button, form turning, boring).
   1. Before you are going to process the workpiece with the ..... you must regulate the speed.
   2. Working at a ..... is difficult for beginners, we need ..... machinists.
   3. We have to be careful with the ..... today, each of these workpieces must get a different profile.
   4. You must change the tool, this one is for ..... holes.

5. The workman at the other machine can cut that round bar steel for you. My machine is set for …… .
6. The ….. are making so much noise that visitors usually leave this room very quickly.

c) Translate the following words into English and fill in the gaps:
(einsetzen, bearbeiten, einstellen, bedienen, anlassen, bohren).
1. You have to ….. the speed.
2. You have to ….. another cutter.
3. Can you ….. two holes, one inch deep?
4. Can't you ….. different lathes?
5. You mustn't ….. this punching machine now
6. You needn't ….. these pieces.

d) How to operate (start – stop) an machine.
Fill in the right words:
1. You ….. a lever.
2. You ….. a knob.
3. You ….. a button.
4. You ….. a switch.

e) Fill in – *some* – *any*:
1. Have you got ….. grease for my machine?
2. No, I haven't, I have only got ….. lubricating oil.
3. Can ….. of you help me to fix the cutter?
4. I can't find ….. spare parts for the lathe.
5. We can punch ….. holes in this plate.
6. We must cut ….. more grooves.

Lesson 4A

A Plumber's Job

Have you ever tried to install a hot water geyser in your kitchen? Let me warn you. It's too much for a d.i.y. enthusiast. Fred Harper tried it the other day. He was sure he could fit all the joints and pipes, but in the end he gave it up and called the plumber.

The plumber's workshop is just round the corner. Whenever he gets a telephone call from one of his neighbours, he knows that a d.i.y. worker is at his wit's end.

Usually he puts things right very quickly, if it is a washer for a tap or a leak somewhere. In his estate car he has his welding and soldering gear, everything he needs for repairs.

A soldering iron to solder pieces of soft metal together, the oxy-acetylene cylinder and his welding torch are part of his welding equipment. Whenever he has to weld pipes or steel plates he protects his eyes from the sparks and the glaring white light with a handshield or with safety goggles.

The welders in a welding shop have to wear helmets and protective clothing of course.

Lesson 4B

The First Steps

Jack Turner's oldest boy, Henry, is happy. The big chemical plant in the town has taken on a number of boys as apprentices.

Henry has just come home after his first day at work. He is still very excited and is telling everyone about it. "We have seen everything! An engineer and a foreman took our group round the plant. We are ten locksmiths and eight plumbers.

They showed us the canteen where we got a drink. They answered all our questions and put us in the picture about our jobs.

At first glance it looks like routine work – all the big tanks, the boilers and the pipe systems. But the foreman said that it is an important job and you are responsible for the work you do. The engineer said that the other workers rely on you and that they need reliable chaps.

But all those indicators – the thermometers, gauges, scales and lamps. One of the chaps said that he would never learn it.

And then the foreman explained that it's just a big system of information. He said he just looks at the scales and needles and he sees at a glance if the temperature has fallen, if the pressure is constant or if there is a leak anywhere.

"Yes, that's right, Henry", his father interrupts. "A friend of mine works at a control system. He says that you develop an instinct, a sixth sense for these things, that's what makes a good workman. And what question did you ask?"

"Well, Dad, I asked what prospects the job had. They said that on the whole they weren't bad. Reliable and experienced locksmiths, plumbers and fitters can get jobs anywhere, at coal mines, steel plants and at the big oil corporations. They pay best. Have you heard how much the chaps on the drilling rigs in the North Sea get?"

"I have, Henry, but they have to work terribly hard to get it".

Exercises 4:

a) You are a plumber and you have got a call from a firm where the central heating and the hot water supply aren't working. You ask the caretaker some questions:
Begin with: a) did you – b) have you – c) haven't you
1. ..... (to check) the indicators?
2. ..... (to check) the water pressure?
3. ..... (to notice) a leak anywhere?
4. ..... (to turn off) the supply at the mains?

b) Translate into German:
1. Can't you find the fault?
2. Doesn't he install new pipes?
3. Haven't you read the operating instructions?
4. Didn't he know that we wear protective helmets?
5. Won't he replace the thermometer?

c) Translate into English:
1. Wir müssen einen Klempner holen.
2. Kennst du dieses neue Heißwassergerät nicht?
3. Wir können den Absperrhahn nicht finden.
4. Dieser Heizkessel funktioniert nicht (to work).

d) Put the right words together to make a sentence. Begin with:
He .....
Example: to protect – eyes = He protects his eyes.
1. to install – the pressure
2. to solder – the washer
3. to wear – the geyser
4. to watch – the wires
5. to change – the safety goggles

e) Fill in the right word:

(pressure – control system – temperature – gauge – needles)

1. The ..... has fallen.
2. The ..... is constant.
3. Watch the red and black ..... on the indicator.
4. The ..... shows that the tank is nearly empty.
5. We must check the whole .....

f) Translate Exercise e) into German:

Lesson 5A

The Exterior of a Motor-Car

1. body – Karosserie
2. chassis – Fahrgestell
3. roof – Dach
4. sliding roof – Schiebedach
5. windscreen – Windschutzscheibe; windscreen wiper – Scheibenwischer
6. windows (side windows, door window) – Fenster
7. (heated) rear window – (heizbare) Heckscheibe
8. wing mirror – Außenrückspiegel; rearview mirror – Rückspiegel
9. door handle – Türgriff
10. lock – Türschloß
11. bonnet – Motorhaube (U.S.: hood)
12. aerial – Antenne
13. boot – Kofferraum (U.S.: trunk); boot lid – Deckel; boot lock – Schloß
14. mudguard – Kotflügel (front, rear, left, right) U.S.: fender
15. radiator grill – Kühlergrill (-gitter) radiator – Kühler

16. number plate – Nummernschild
17. licence number – Zulassungsnummer
18. headlights – Scheinwerfer (dipped beam – Abblendlicht; full beam – Fernlicht; parking light – Standlicht)
19. fog lights – Nebelleuchte; rear fog light – Nebelschlußleuchte
20. rear lights – Rückleuchten (Rücklichter)
21. brake lights – Bremslichter
22. reversing light – Rückfahrscheinwerfer
23. trafficator – Blinker (Fahrtrichtungsanzeiger) (front, rear, left, right)
24. bumper (front, rear) – Stoßstange
25. horn – Hupe
26. wheel – Rad
27. hub cap – Radkappe
28. rim – Felge
29. tyre (U.S.: tire) – Reifen (tubeless t.) – schlauchlos
30. valve (to inflate the tyre) – Ventil zum Aufpumpen des Reifens
31. valve cap – Ventilkappe, -verschluß
32. exhaust pipe – Auspuffrohr
33. silencer – Auspufftopf
34. petrol cap – Tankklappe

Lesson 5B

The Interior of a Motor-Car

1. dashboard – Armaturenbrett
2. speedometer – Tachometer
3. odometer – Kilometerzähler
4. fuel gauge – Kraftstoffanzeiger
5. temperature gauge – Temperaturanzeiger

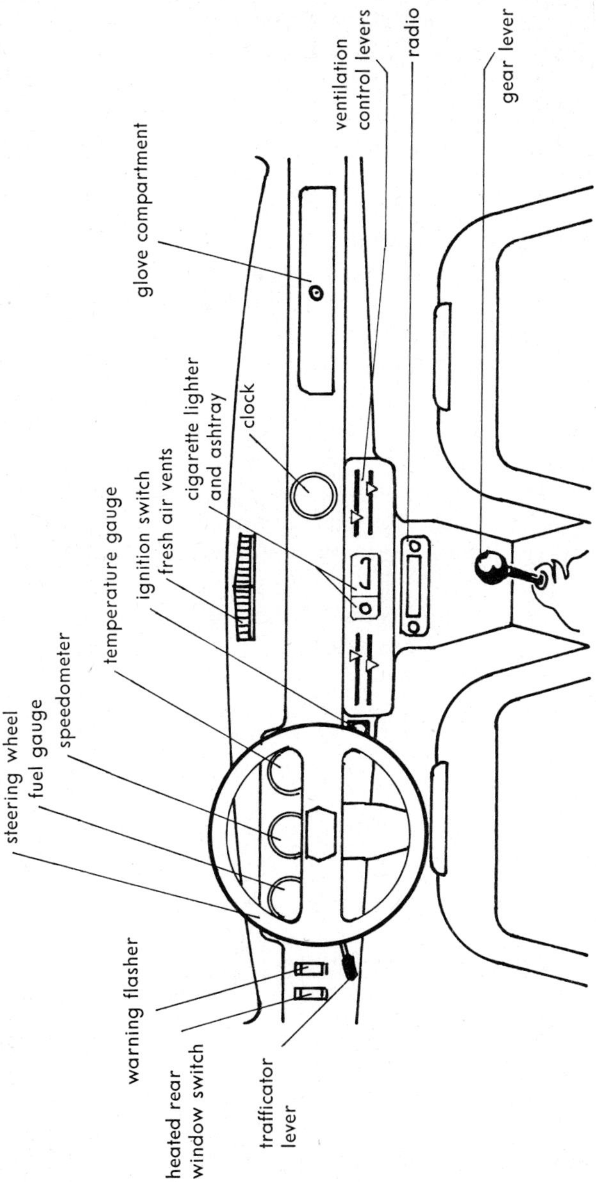
heated rear window switch
trafficator lever
warning flasher
steering wheel
fuel gauge
speedometer
temperature gauge
ignition switch
fresh air vents
cigarette lighter and ashtray
clock
glove compartment
ventilation control levers
radio
gear lever

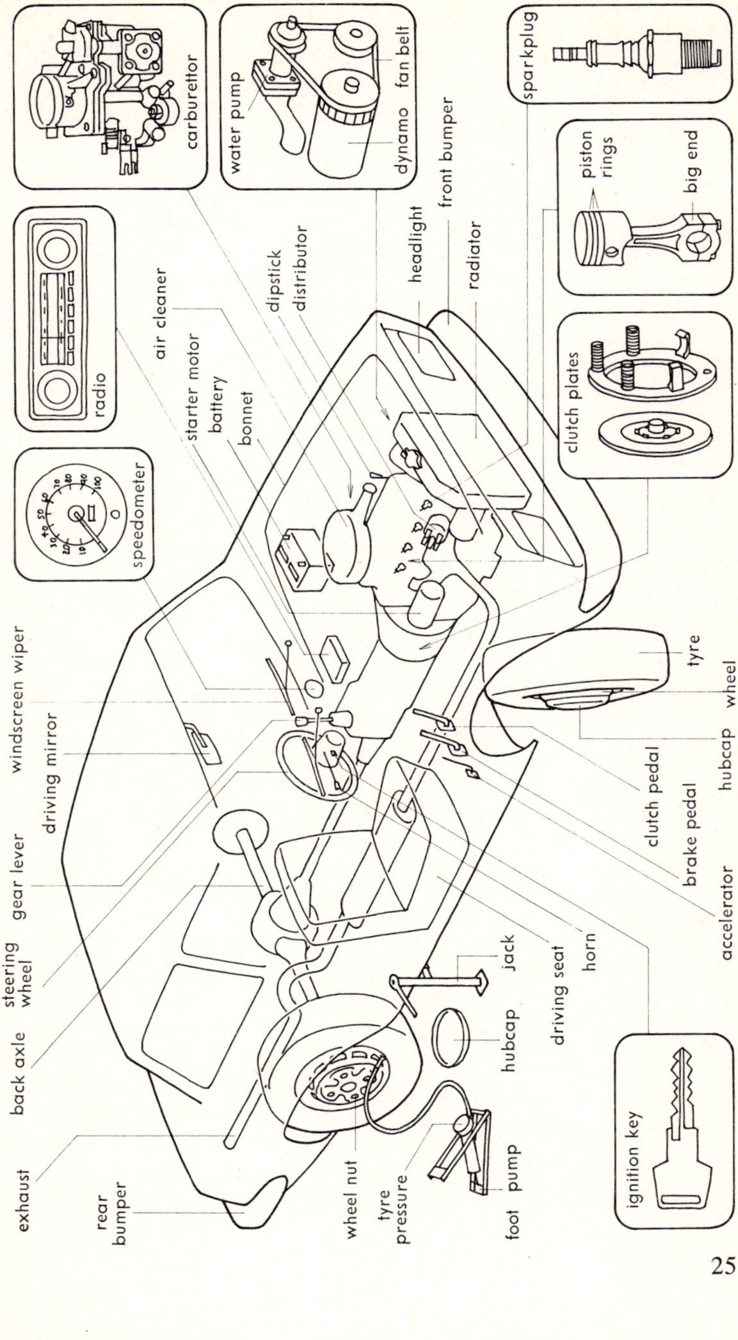
carburettor
water pump
dynamo
fan belt
sparkplug
piston rings
big end
clutch plates
radio
speedometer
front bumper
headlight
radiator
dipstick
distributor
air cleaner
starter motor
battery
bonnet
windscreen wiper
driving mirror
gear lever
steering wheel
back axle
exhaust
rear bumper
tyre
wheel
hubcap
clutch pedal
brake pedal
accelerator
horn
driving seat
jack
hubcap
wheel nut
tyre pressure
foot pump
ignition key

6. oil pressure gauge – Öldruckmesser
7. warning lights (5 and 6) – Kontrolleuchten
8. ignition light (generator warning light) – Lichtmaschinen-anzeiger
9. headlight and dashboard light switch – Schalter-Knopf für Scheinwerfer und Armaturenbrettbeleuchtung
10. ventilation control lever – Lüftungsregulierungshebel
11. fresh air vents – Lüftungsschlitze
12. heater (switch) – Heizungsknopf (schalter)
13. fan – Gebläse
14. steering wheel – Lenkrad
15. horn – Hupe (Ring, Knopf)
16. clock – Uhr
17. adjusting knob (clock) – Stellknopf – Regulierknopf
18. radio – Radio
19. trafficator lever – Blinkerhebel
20. windscreen wiper lever – Scheibenwischerhebel
21. warning flasher – Warnblinkleuchte
22. manual choke – Starterklappe
23. fog light switch – Schalter für Nebelleuchten
24. rear fog light switch – Schalter für Nebelschlußleuchte
25. heated rear window switch – Schalter für beheizte Heck-scheibe
26. inside rear-view mirror – Innenrückspiegel
27. bonnet catch release – Hebel (Zug) zur Entriegelung der Motorhaube
28. petrol cap release – Hebel (Zug) zur Entriegelung der Tankklappe
29. ashtray – Aschenbecher
30. glove compartment – Handschuhfach
31. ignition switch – Zündschloß; ignition key – Zündschlüssel
32. gear lever – Ganghebel
33. accelerator pedal – Gaspedal
34. brake pedal – Bremspedal
35. clutch pedal – Kupplungspedal
36. handbrake – Handbremse
37. seats (front, rear) – Sitze

38. driver's seat – Fahrersitz
passenger seat – Beifahrersitz
39. window handle – Kurbel
40. arm rest – Armstütze
41. head rest – Kopfstütze
42. seat belt – Gurt
43. seat belt buckle – Gurtverriegelung

Exercises 5:

a) Find the right words from the list to fill the gaps:
(ventilation – heater – rear-view mirror – seat belts – boot – mudguard – starter – fuel gauge – speedometer – bumper – headlights)
1. It's rather dark, turn on the .....
2. Look at the .....; you mustn't drive too fast.
3. The ..... is on reserve, the tank is nearly empty.
4. It wasn't so bad when I hit the tree; just a dent on the front .....
5. Don't forget to fasten the ..... before you start.

b) Fred Harper is leaving for his holidays. His wife is asking him if the car is ready.
Example: water – to put – radiator (Have you put water in the radiator yet?) Now you ask the questions:
Have ..... yet?
1. road maps – to put – glove compartment
2. to change – left front tyre
3. to adjust – headlights
4. to check – air pressure – in the spare wheel
5. to fix – seat belts – on the rear seats

c) Something is wrong with Fred's car. Try to put it right.
1. He opens the bonnet to take out his driving licence.
2. He turns the window handle to start the car.
3. He looks at the speedometer to see the cars behind him.
4. He turns on the parking light because it is raining.
5. He pulls the oil pressure gauge to stop the car.

d) Translate a), b), c) into German:

Lesson 6A

Driving a Car

1. Put the key in the ignition.
2. Make sure the car is in neutral (neutral gear).
3. Turn the key clockwise to start the engine.
4. Release the key immediately when you hear that the engine has started.
5. If the engine is cold pull out the choke, but push it in as soon as it is running smoothly.
6. Fasten your seat belt.
7. Put your left foot on the clutch pedal, depress it and put the car into first or reverse gear.
8. Put your right foot on the brake pedal and release the hand-brake.
9. Look in the rear-view mirror and over your shoulder to see if anything is coming.
10. Switch on the trafficator to signal that you are going to move off.
11. Put your right foot on the accelerator pedal.
12. Release the clutch slowly and accelerate gently.
13. If you have to reverse the car and you can't see what is behind you, ask somebody to guide you.
14. As the car gathers speed, you change up into second, third, fourth gear.

Lesson 6B

Trouble With a New Car

Jack: "Hallo, Fred! How's the new car?"
Fred: "Oh, don't ask about that. I've had nothing but trouble with it".
Jack: "Oh, what's wrong with it?"
Fred: "Well, three days after I bought it the windscreen wipers stopped working. I took it to the garage and they put in a new fuse. But on my way home the oil pressure light came on".
Jack: "Didn't you have enough oil in the engine?"
Fred: "Of course I had. A new car doesn't use up oil so quickly. Anyway, when it was fixed, all the lights on the dashboard went out".

Jack: "Oh, that's dangerous! I remember I had the same trouble with my car last winter. You feel absolutely helpless!"

Fred: "How right you are! I couldn't see the speedometer and was driving too quickly. The police stopped me and I got a fine for speeding".

Jack: "Well, you've got new bulbs for the dashboard and it's all right now, isn't it?"

Fred: "That's what I said to myself this morning, and on the way to my office I ran out of petrol".

Jack: "Blimey! I suppose the petrol gauge wasn't working, was it?"

Fred: "Exactly! It showed that the tank was still a quarter full".

Jack: "And where is the car now?"

Fred: "In the garage. Tomorrow morning I'm going to ride to the office on my son's bike".

Exercises 6:

a) Fill in the missing words:

1. When you turn the ignition key you hear the .....
2. Make sure that the car is in ..... gear.
3. Put your foot on the ..... pedal when you change gear.
4. Look in the ..... before you overtake another car.
5. You put your foot on the ..... pedal and the car goes faster.
6. You put your foot on the ..... pedal to slow down.
7. You signal with the ..... and turn off to the right or left.

b) Fill in the right words, but check the tense:
(to put – to make – to release – to go – to change)

1. Before he moves off the driver ..... the handbrake.
2. Yesterday all the lights ..... out, I couldn't see anything.
3. The mechanic is ..... in a new fuse.
4. Yes, the road is bad, I ..... just ..... down into second gear.

5. I ..... sure that nothing was coming before I moved off.
6. We ..... in the new radio next week.

c) Make words from the words in list A and B:
Example: ignition key (ignition key)

A.	B.
1. rear view	1. wipers
2. accelerator	2. brake
3. oil	3. pipe
4. fuel	4. mirror
5. hand	5. gauge
6. windscreen	6. pedal
7. exhaust	7. pressure

d) Finish the sentences:
(two questions; two negative questions; two negative statements)
Example: Why ..... you put your foot on the accelerator pedal when you released the clutch?
(Why didn't you put .....?)
1. ..... you buy new windscreen wipers last week?
2. When ..... you lose your key?
3. I ..... clean the rear window when I started.
4. .... they check the oil level at the service station?
5. I ..... know that there are new traffic lights at our corner.
6. Why ..... you turn on the lights when you were entering the tunnel?

Lesson 7A

Buying a Second-Hand Car

Car dealer: "What about this car? It's only four years old and has a reconditioned engine with a six-month-guarantee".

Customer: "What's the fuel consumption like?"

Car dealer: "About 30 miles a gallon in normal traffic".

Customer: "What about regular maintenance?"

Car dealer: "We serviced it last week. We adjusted the brakes and fitted new front tyres".

Customer: "What about extras?"

Car dealer: "Well, it has a car radio and seat belts".

Customer: "Can I have a test drive?"

Car dealer: "Certainly".

Customer: (After the test drive) "Not bad. The brakes are all right, but I think the steering is a bit slack".

Car dealer: "We can have a look at that if you like".

Customer: "Yes, and the accelerator is a bit stiff".

Car dealer: "No problem. It just needs a few drops of oil".

Customer: "How much are you asking for it?"

Car dealer: "£550. It's a bargain at the price".

Customer: "All right, I'll take it if you put those things right first."

Car dealer: "Of course. All our cars leave us in perfect running order".

Lesson 7B

How to Change a Wheel

Jack Turner's wife has been very lucky. It's the first time that a tyre on her car has got a puncture but it happened only a few hundred yards away from their house.
At the moment her son Henry is changing the wheel.
Let us see what he is doing:
He is taking off the hub cap with a big screwdriver; he is loosening the nuts with a wheel spanner.
Now he is fixing a car jack under the chassis.
He must jack up the car a bit and take off the nuts.
The wheel comes off quickly.
He has already taken out the spare wheel and is fitting it on the bolts.
Now he is putting on the nuts again and is screwing them on a bit with his hands.
Now he is letting the car down and is tightening the nuts crosswise.
Finally he puts on the hub cap again.

Exercises 7:

a) Here are the car dealer's answers. You are the customer. What have you asked him?

1. Yes, the engine is new.
2. Of course you can, but you must show me your driving licence.
3. We adjusted the brakes only a few days ago.
4. No, we don't sell car radios.
5. You had better use super in this engine, it's better than regular petrol.

b) Fill in the gaps:
(have – has – hasn't – haven't – yet – already)
Example: ..... the mechanic changed the wheels .....?
(Hasn't the mechanic changed the wheels yet?)

1. We ..... checked the engine.
2. No, I'm afraid the mechanic ..... put in the radio .....
3. ..... you fitted the new winter tyres .....?
4. We ..... serviced this car ..... We will do it after lunch.
5. The customer ..... come back from the test drive.

c) Mrs Turner is proud of her son. She is telling a neighbour how quickly Henry changed the wheel last week.
"Well, really, Mrs Smith, he did it as if he was an experienced mechanic.
First he took off the hub cap with .....
(Study Lesson 7B carefully and finish what Mrs Turner said – past tense! Now = then; must = had to; ask your teacher to check your exercise)

d) Answer these questions:
(Use short forms)
Example: Do you sell second-hand cars? No, ...
(No, I don't)

1. Did you service the car last week? Yes, ...
2. Did they let you keep the new car radio? No, ...
3. Does your friend sell winter tyres? No, ...
4. Will you help me to change the wheels? No, ...
5. Will you check the brakes? Yes, ...

Lesson 8A

At The Garage

Motorist: "Good morning. I wonder if you could have a look at my car".

Mechanic: "Certainly sir. What's the trouble?"

Motorist: "I'm not quite sure. It won't start. We had to push it to start the engine".

Mechanic: "Perhaps the battery is flat. I'll have a look". (The mechanic tries to start the car) "When did you last have your car serviced?"

Motorist: "I can't remember. I sometimes forget to have it serviced."

(About an hour later) "How are you getting on?"

Mechanic: "Finished. Your car is in perfect running order again".

Motorist: "Good. What was wrong with it?"

Mechanic: "Well, you needed new plugs (sparking plugs) for a start and then new points (contact breaker points); so I changed them. The timing was out and I had to adjust it. I cleaned the carburettor, too".

Motorist: "And what about the battery?"

Mechanic: "It's all right. It will charge itself when you drive. But you mustn't forget to keep it topped up with distilled water. You must check it every week, as well as the oil level in your engine and the air pressure in your tyres".

Motorist: "Well, thanks very much for your help".

Mechanic: "Not at all. You can pay inside. The attendant will give you a receipt. But don't leave it so long until the next service."

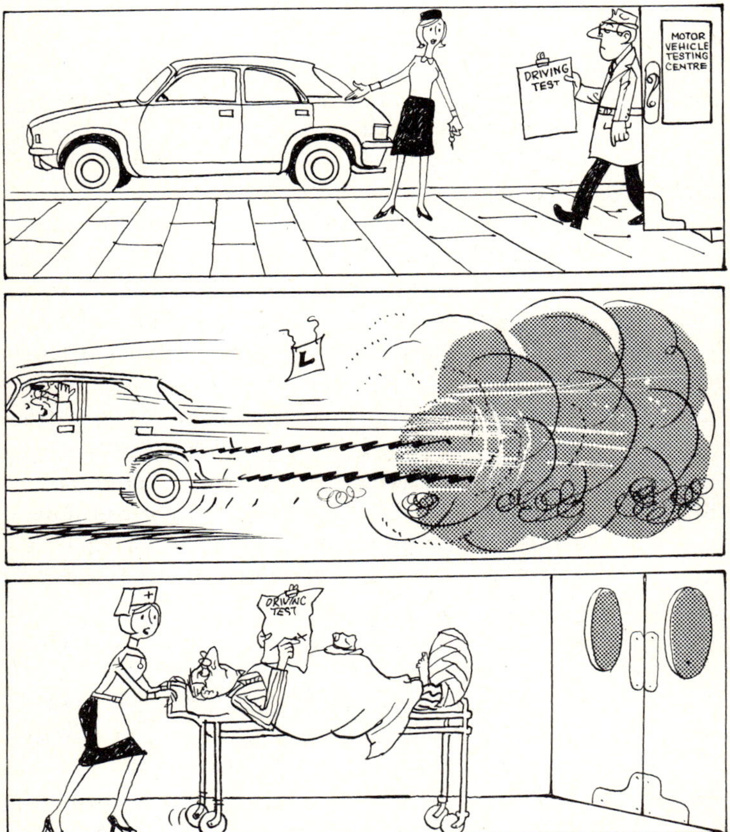

Lesson 8B

The Driving Licence

Jack Turner: "Hallo, Jane! Congratulations! I hear you've passed your driving test".

Jane Harper: "That's right, thanks. And here's my brand-new driving licence".

Jack: "Well, good luck on the road. When did you take the test?"

Jane: "Yesterday".

Jack: "Was it very difficult?"

Jane: "Not really. Learning to drive was the problem. It took me several lessons to get used to the car and to the heavy traffic in the city centre".

Jack: "Well, don't worry. It's always a bit difficult at first. After a few months you'll react instinctively".

Jane: "Yes, I hope so; but I'm still afraid of driving through the city during the rush hours with all these reckless drivers. Traffic makes me nervous. Can't you give me a few practical hints?"

Jack: "Well, statistics show that a lot of accidents happen at road junctions, so drive cautiously and watch out for all the traffic lights. Give way, when other cars have the right of way. Don't overtake at pedestrian crossings or on a bend or when you are approaching the brow of a hill".

Jane: "Now, really, Jack! You sound like the 'Highway Code'".

Jack: "Well, it's all good common sense. Also, don't start off too quickly and watch out for elderly people and children crossing the road".

Jane: "What a lot to think about! And you speak of instinctive reactions. I wonder if I will ever become a good driver”.

Jack: “Don’t worry. It’s just a matter of time. In a year you’ll be an experienced driver”.

Exercises 8:

a) A policeman is telling a reckless driver about his mistakes. Choose the right words to fill the gaps:
(parked – without – have to – drove – overtook – didn’t – haven’t – made)

1. You ..... stop at the traffic lights when they are red.
2. You ..... parked at the right place.
3. Your car ..... such a noise when you started off.
4. ..... you see the pedestrians at the crossing?
5. You turned off to the right ..... giving a signal.
6. You ..... two cars on a bend; that’s dangerous.
7. You ..... your car here longer than ten minutes.
8. You ..... too fast; there’s a speed limit sign.

b) Translate into English:

1. Fahre nicht zu schnell; siehst du nicht die Kinder?
2. Du darfst nicht überholen, es sind zwei Busse vor dir.
3. Siehst du nicht das Zeichen für Geschwindigkeitsbegrenzung?
4. Du mußt jetzt die Geschwindigkeit verringern. (to slow down)
5. Warum hast du angehalten? Die Ampel (engl. Mehrzahl) ist grün.
6. Du brauchst nicht anzuhalten, du hast Vorfahrt.
7. Du darfst nicht losfahren, die Straßenkreuzung ist noch nicht frei. (clear)

c) Answer these questions:

1. Why won't many engines start on a cold winter morning?
2. What must a motorist check from time to time to keep his car in running order?
3. What liquids (Flüssigkeit) do you have to put in the tank, the engine, the battery?
4. Why must you slow down at crossings and road junctions?
5. Why don't learners like driving during rush hours?

d) A learner comes back from his first drive without a teacher. He is still very nervous and tells his friends what happened: (Fill in – have to – has to – had to – will have to = müssen)

1. You know, every driver ..... turn on the lights in heavy rain and I forgot that.
2. I was very nervous when I ..... reverse the car.
3. Then I ..... stop at nearly all the traffic lights and two times I stalled the engine.
4. The teacher always said: "You ..... drive to the right (Engl. left) when another car is going to overtake you", and I didn't do that.
5. Tomorrow I ..... to drive to the station to meet my sister, but my brother ..... come with me; he is a better driver than I am.

e) Translate d) into German:

Lesson 9A

Motorways

Fred Harper has just returned from a trip to the continent and is telling his friends about German motorways.

Jack: "And what are the German motorways like?"

Fred: "They're not very different from ours. Of course, they drive on the right, so you have to overtake on the left".

Betty: "Isn't that confusing?"

Fred: "Just at first. But you get used to it. You just follow all the other traffic".

Jack: "Do they have a speed limit on German motorways?"

Fred: "Not usually. Only where there are roadworks for resurfacing and so on. The official recommendation is – do not exceed 130 kmh – that's about 80 mph."

Betty: "How many lanes do they have?"

Fred: "Well, as you know, the Germans had their first motorways a long time before we had ours, so many of them have only two lanes and the hard shoulders are quite narrow. The new ones have three lanes, like ours.
Most other things are the same as here. You are not allowed to stop or turn and there are patrol cars, (police and road service – ADAC) and telephones along the motorway in case you have a breakdown. But it is expensive if you have to get a tow to the nearest garage".

Jack: "So there's not much difference then".

Fred: "No, not really. Except for the helicopters. We don't see them very often. In Germany, during the rush hours or when there is a traffic jam or an accident, the police helicopters patrol above the motorways".

Lesson 9B

Information about Motorways

A motorway is a road which is divided into two parts (carriageways) so that traffic travelling in different directions is kept apart.
You drive on to a motorway at an access point.
You drive off at an exit.
Each carriageway usually has two or three lanes.
The third lane is for lorries with trailers and long vehicles which are slow in hilly regions.
There are places along the motorway where you can drive off to get petrol, to have the car serviced, have something to eat or drink or stay the night (motels).
There are also special parking areas or lay-bys for picnics.
The speed limit is 70 mph – about 110 kmh on British motorways, in Germany a speed limit of 130 kmh is recommended.
Motorways are fast and safe but sometimes there are dreadful accidents.
The most frequent causes are bad overtaking, driving too close to the vehicle in front, driving too fast when the lane is wet and falling asleep at the wheel.

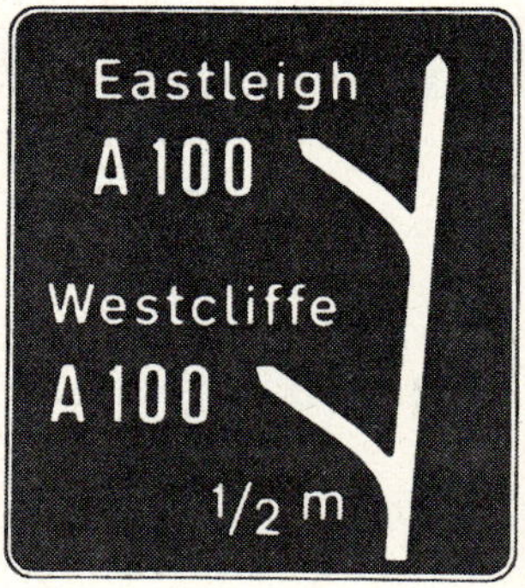

Exercises 9:

a) Fill in the missing verbs. Choose seven words from this list: (to see – to watch – to fill – to look – to study – to drive – to slow down – to check – to repair – to change – to overlook – to overtake).

1. ..... your speed when you are on a motorway.
2. At the service station the attendant will ..... your tank and ..... the oil level and the air pressure.
3. You must ..... when you see the speed limit sign.
4. Remember that you must ..... in the rear-view mirror.
5. You must accelerate when you are going to ..... another car.
6. When there is an accident, drivers must ..... lanes and drive past carefully.

b) Make sentences: Perfect tense – with I. yet (question) II. not yet (negative statement) III. already (positive statement).

Example: to check the tyres

I. Has the driver checked the tyres yet?

II. No, he hasn't checked them yet.

III. Yes, he has already checked them.

1. to buy a road map;
2. to fill the tank;
3. to reach the end of the speed limit;
4. to overtake the lorry;
5. to pass the roadworks;
6. to change into first gear;

c) Put in prepositions (for – at – on – with – to)

1. The motorist stopped ..... the motorway.
2. He could not give an answer ..... the policeman's questions.
3. The policeman waited ..... another policeman who could speak French.
4. The driver said that he had overlooked a speed limit sign ..... the access point.
5. The policeman spoke ..... him for some time.
6. He let him go ..... a warning.

d) Now try to make six questions from exercise c)

Begin the questions with (where – why – what – when)

Example: Why did the motorist stop?

Lesson 10A

Combustion Engine – Four Stroke Engine

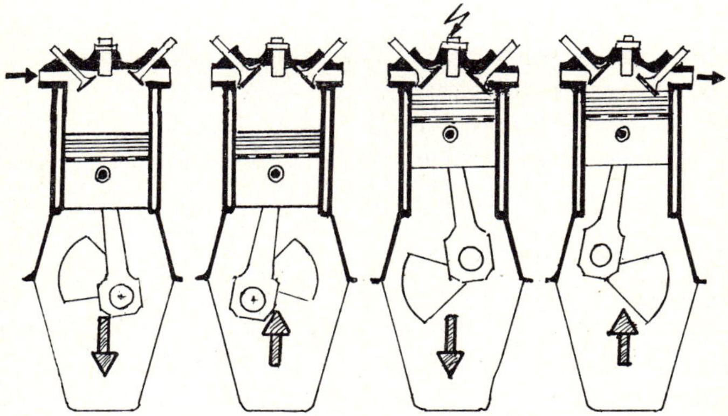

1. Stroke – Induction
Petrol and air are mixed in the carburettor. The piston moves down and this explosive gas is drawn into the cylinder through the inlet valve. The outlet valve is closed.
2. Stroke – Compression
Inlet and outlet valve are closed; the piston goes up and the gas is compressed in the combustion chamber.
3. Stroke – Ignition
The valves are closed. The sparking plug ignites the gas. The power of the explosion drives the piston down.
4. Stroke – Exhaust
The piston goes up again. The inlet valve is closed, the outlet valve is open to let the exhaust gas out.

Lesson 10B

At a Car Assembly Plant

Personnel Manager: "So you want to make some money here before you begin your next term? Well, we pay good wages but we demand hard work, discipline and perseverance. Do you think you can work on the assembly line?"

Student: "Well, yes, I know a lot about cars. I usually check and repair my car myself and help my friends with their cars and mopeds".

Personnel Manager: "All right, it will be easier for you as you like repairing cars, but you'll see that the jobs here can be very dull".

Student: "I've heard about that. And what exactly must I do?"

Personnel Manager: "The foreman will tell you. I suppose you'll have a job on the main line, tightening nuts with a spanner or a power wrench".

Student: "I see. The body of the car is on the main line and the other parts, wheels, bumpers etc. are fitted there?"

Personnel Manager: "That's right. The hoists lift the different parts on to the line and the workers assemble the car. But you must keep up with the pace of the line, if you are tightening nuts, putting in rear-view mirrors, spot welding or anything else. The line must not stop."

Student: "And if I have to leave my place for a few minutes?"

Personnel Manager: "You press a button and another worker will come to take your place. Now you'd better report to the foreman. Your work begins with the afternoon shift. Good luck!"

Exercises 10:

a) Answer these questions:
1. What is the function of the sparking plugs in the engine?
2. What happens in the carburettor?
3. When are both outlet and inlet valve closed?
4. How does the burnt gas leave the car?
5. How does the electric power go to the sparking plugs?
6. How can car plants produce hundreds of cars every day?
7. What do they demand of their workers?
8. Why do many people say that work at a car plant is very dull?
9. Why don't we use battery cars yet instead of motor cars?

(Find several answers to question nr. 9)

b) Say what the new worker does and put in the right word: (Choose 4 words from this list – to learn – to change – to sell – to operate – to fit – to check).
Begin with: The new worker .....
1. The new worker ..... the rear-view mirrors.
2. The new worker ..... to work with spot welding equipment.
3. The new worker ..... the hoist.
4. The new worker ..... the trafficators.

c) Change your sentences exercise b) first into questions, then into negative statements.

d) Now you can test yourself on what you know about car production and car models.
Fill in the country and the names of the models:

Country	Models
VW is a German plant	They produce Golf, Passat …
Leyland is a …..	They produce …..
Renault	
Chrysler	
Ford	
General Motors	
Opel	
Toyota	
Rolls Royce	
Volvo	
Fiat	
Saab Scania	
Peugeot	
Mercedes	

Lesson 11A

As Many as Possible

The Harpers are going to renovate their house. At the moment they hardly ever talk about anything else.
Fred has just come home and Jane is telling him about her visit to the architect.

Jane: "Well, the architect agrees with me".

Fred: "What about?"

Jane: "About the wall sockets of course. He says we should have as many as possible. We will need at least four in the kitchen. And then we will need two lamps with 60 and 100 watt bulbs and a fluorescent light for the ceiling".

Fred: "All right. But this is the last time we change our plans. Have you any more suggestions?"

Jane: "Just an idea. I'll need a special cupboard with shelves for all my electric appliances".

Fred: "What appliances?"

Jane: "The foodmixer, the toaster, the egg boiler ....."

Fred: "Wait a minute. If you're going to be using all those appliances at the same time, as well as the dishwasher, fridge, deepfreezer and cooker, then we'd better check with the architect again. We don't want to overload the circuit. Perhaps we'll need a special circuit and another distribution box and extra fuses for the kitchen".

Jane: "Well, I don't know much about all these technical details".

Fred: "I'm no expert either. Anyway, we can ask the electrician tomorrow when he installs the fluorescent light".

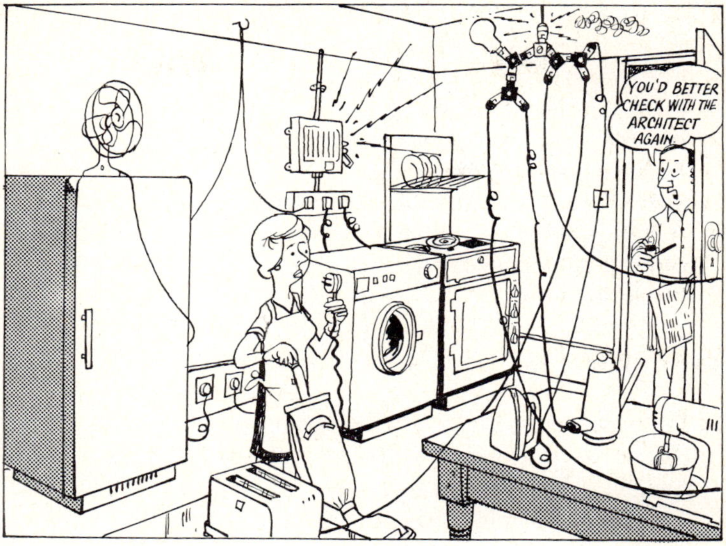

Lesson 11B

Simple Repairs

Do it yourself enthusiasts can cope with simple electrical problems, but if you are not sure, you should call an electrician.

Always switch off the electricity at the mains before you start to do any electrical repairs.

If you want to fit a new light you should check the wires in the ceiling. They are attached to a terminal block with two clamps for each wire. Loosen the tiny screws in the terminal block, strip the sheathing off the ends of the wires, put the ends in the terminal block and tighten the screws. Make sure that there are no loose strands of wire touching. Put a bulb in and switch on the light.

4 Pocketbook of Technical English (40551)

Basic Tool Kit for Minor Repairs

1. Electrician's screwdriver
2. Pliers with insulated handles
3. A torch – preferably plastic – or rubber-covered
4. A sharp pocket knife
5. Spare fuses for plugs, fuse wire and automatic fuses
6. A wire stripper – you can adjust it to remove insulation without damaging the wire
7. Insulating tape

Exercises 11:

a) Fill in the gaps. Choose the words from the following list: (fridge – dishwasher – fluorescent light – ideas – wall sockets – deep-freezer – cooker – electrician)
   1. This ..... is much brighter than ordinary lights.
   2. The electric ..... should be near the window to let the steam out
   3. Be careful with ice cream. Don't put it in the ....., put it in the .....
   4. I haven't put the plates in the cupboard yet, they are still in the .....
   5. Very often you can find some useful ..... in this family magazine.
   6. The ..... is coming to install two new .....

b) Translate the sentences in exercise a) into German:

c) Complete the sentences (use question tags and ask the teacher to help you).
   Example: You won't do that ..... ? (You won't do that, will you?)
   We'll need another wall socket .....? (We'll need another wall socket, won't we?)
   1. You are going to see the architect, ...?
   2. We don't want to overload the circuit, ...?

3. He knows a lot about electricity, ...?
4. We can ask the electrician, ...?
5. They don't talk about anything else, ...?

d) Compare electrical appliances:
(as – as; not as – as; ..... than)
Example: fluorescent light – bulb (bright) (The f. light is *brighter than* the bulb.
1. Food mixer – toaster; (expensive)
2. Deepfreezer – fridge; (good)
3. Plastic covered torch – rubber covered torch; (cheap)
4. Mechanic's screwdriver – electrician's screwdriver (big)

Lesson 12A

Electricity in the Home

After the electrician had installed the fluorescent light at the Harper's, Fred and Jane asked him to explain to them about domestic electricity and electric currents. Here are some of the things they learned:
1. The usual current for domestic circuits is a.c. (alternating current) with a voltage of 240 volts (Germ. 220). In factories d.c. (direct current) is sometimes used as well as three-phase current and power current.
2. When you switch on a light you complete an electric circuit. You break the circuit when you switch the light off.
3. Several domestic appliances, for example electric heaters, use so much electricity that they need a special circuit so that the system is not overloaded. Apart from the consumption of current it is annoying when there is a short circuit and the lights go out. This is because a fuse has blown. A fuse is the weakest part of the circuit. It will blow as soon as the circuit is overloaded. This protection is very important. Without it the wires would get hot and catch fire.

4. What do you do when a fuse has blown? Turn off the appliance and check the fuse box. In Britain, small electrical appliances also have a fuse in their plugs. Check this first and replace it if it has blown.
The other fuses are in the fuse box. In Britain they have to be rewired . Switch off the electricity at the mains, take out the fuse and rewire it with the correct wire, 5 amp (ampere) for lights circuits, 10 or 15 amp for power circuits and 30 amp for large fixed appliances. In Germany it is easier. The fuses switch off automatically if the circuit is overloaded. Check the fuse box. If the small button in the fuse has come out, just push it back in again.

Lesson 12B

How Electricity Works

Electricity flows only when it can complete a circuit. Domestic electric cables have two or three wires. Electricity flows along the live wire from the source of power to the appliance and then back along the neutral wire.
We have a short circuit when the electricity can flow directly from the live wire to the neutral wire without passing through an appliance.
The third, the earth wire, is connected to the exposed metalwork of all appliances. In a shrouded contact plug it has contact with a thin metal plate.
Each of the wires has a different colour.

Exercises 12:

a) Form questions:
   1. The electrician checked the fuse box first.
   (What ..... ?)
   2. The lights went out between seven and eight o'clock
   (When ..... ?)
   3. The shop assistant put the spare bulbs in the bag.
   (Where ..... ?)
   4. He gave the customer some insulating tape.
   (What ..... ?)
   5. We bought two new lights for the workshop.
   (How many ..... ?)

b) Fill in the verbs. Be careful to choose the right form:
   1. The housewife has ..... the mixer.(to turn off)
   2. The circuit was ..... (to complete)

3. We didn't know that the wire was ..... (to break)
4. The wires can be ..... (to install)
5. We have ..... a lot of electrical appliances.(to sell)

c) Fill in the correct prepositions. Choose from this list: (on – in – at – between – out – off – under – of – into – with)
   1. Connect the ends ..... the wires.
   2. Turn ..... the electric current before you pull .... the wires.
   3. Put the plug ..... the wall socket now.
   4. You can find ..... the voltage if you look .... the little plate ..... the back of the appliance.
   5. Ask an electrician when you have problems ..... your cooker.

d) Some days ago you installed a lamp in your study. Translate into English what you had to do: (Begin each sentence with: I had to .....)
   1. nach der Verteilerdose suchen, (to look for)
   2. eine Leitung (wire) längs der Wand legen,
   3. Lüsterklemmen an (on) den Enden der Leitung anbringen,
   4. die Leitung in der Verteilerdose mit dem elektrischen Gerät verbinden,
   5. ein Loch in die Wand bohren,
   6. einen Mauerdübel für einen Haken (hook) reinstecken (to put in),
   7. die Lampe anbringen (befestigen),
   8. eine Birne in die Fassung drehen (to put in).

Lesson 13A

Buying Some Equipment at the Electrical Shop

Jack: "I'd like some light switches, please".

Assistant: "Certainly, sir. I expect you want rocker switches, don't you?"

Jack: "Yes, please. And I think I'll need a special switch for the bathroom. I looked up the word yesterday in my do-it-yourself book but I have forgotten it again".

Assistant: "Do you mean a pull-cord switch? It has a shock-proof cord so that you can't touch the switch with your hands. With wet hands you could get a shock".

Jack: "Yes, that's it. And then I'll need an extension lead for the table lamp in my study".

Assistant: "Yes. I can give you an extension flex. It has a cable socket at one end for the lamp plug and a plug at the other end for the socket on the wall".

Jack: "Thanks. There's one more problem. We haven't got enough socket outlets in our kitchen. My wife needs some more for her electrical appliances".

Assistant: "That's no problem. You just need a socket panel. You plug it into a normal socket outlet and that gives you three or four additional power outlets".

Jack: "That's a good idea. We hadn't thought of that. Right. That's all for now, thank you".

Assistant: "Well, sir, you never know when you might have to do a small repair job. Here's our brochure with a complete list of all our prices of appliances and fittings, switches, plugs and other accessories. There's also some good advice for the do-it-yourself man. It tells you how to mend a fuse and wire a plug, the basic rules about electricity, how to switch off the electricity at the mains and so on".

Jack: "Thanks. I'm sure it will come in handy in our house".

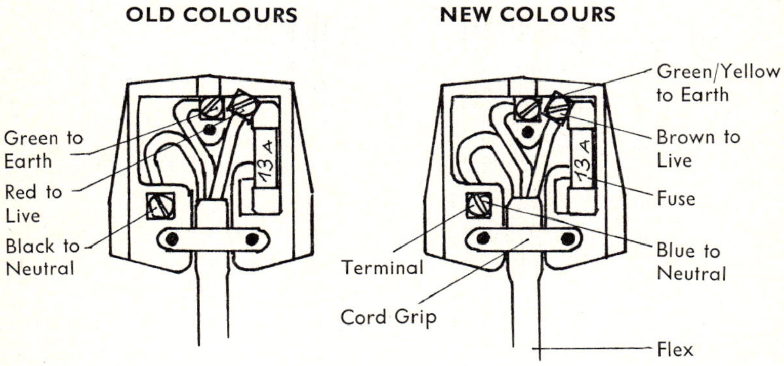

Lesson 13B

How to Wire a Plug

In Britain, most plugs have three pins for the neutral, live and earth connections. They are fitted with 13 amp size fuses.

To wire a three-pin plug:

1. Loosen the main screw to open the plug.
2. Loosen the screws holding the cord grip.
3. Unscrew the three terminal screws.
4. Cut each wire so that it will reach the correct terminal.
5. Strip enough covering from the wires so that they can be wound round the terminals.
6. Wind the bare wires round the terminals: brown (or red) – Live – round the terminal on the right; blue (or black) – Neutral – round the left-hand terminal; green = yellow – Earth – round the top terminal. (different colours in Germany)

7. Make sure there are no stray ends of wire, then screw back the terminal screws.
8. Make sure the cord grip holds the flex firmly, then screw on the plug cover.

Exercises 13:

a) You are buying some electrical appliances.
Ask the assistant:
   1. if he has any light switches,
   2. if he has a price list for electrical accessories,
   3. if they sell socket panels,
   4. if they send an electrician to install appliances,
   5. if they can come at weekends to do urgent repairs.

b) Find the missing word:
   1. The cord on a pull-cord switch is ..... so that you don't get a ..... if you touch it with wet hands.
   2. The nearest socket ..... is in the corridor. We'll need an ..... lead to reach it.
   3. This socket panel will give you four ..... power .....
   4. Don't forget to switch off the electricity at the ..... before you start work.
   5. When you wire a plug, wind the ..... round the correct ..... and make sure there are no stray ..... .

c) Fill in – already – yet – still:
   1. Have you got your new mixer .....?
   2. Yes, but the children are ..... trying it out, so I haven't used it .....
   3. But you haven't paid for it .....!
   4. I know. The electrician is ..... busy with the washing machine. Something is wrong with it. Can't you give him the money?
   5. I'm afraid I can't. I've ..... told the shop assistant that I'll pay tomorrow morning.

d) Study this dialogue and fill in:
(some – much – more – few – a few – a lot of – little – many)

Jane Harper and Betty Turner are going to buy some electrical equipment at the supermarket.

Jane: "Betty, can't you help me? There are so ..... plugs here, but I don't see any three-pin-plugs."

Betty: "Well, I've just seen ..... in a box on the shelf on the other side".

Jane: "And there isn't anybody to help us".

Betty: "Well, on Monday mornings, with only .... customers in the shop there are always ..... of assistants and they have ..... of time for you. But right now on Friday afternoon when everybody is in a hurry and doesn't have ..... time, we have to help ourselves".

Jane: "I think we'd better come again tomorrow morning. We'll have ..... time then. I have to buy ..... fuses and terminal blocks anyway.
There are too ..... customers here now, we have ..... chance of getting home quickly".

e) Translate exercise d) into German:

Lesson 14A

Unwelcome Neighbours

The Turners at the breakfast table:

Betty: "Jack, here's something in the paper which is more interesting than the sports news. It seems to be definite now that they are going to build a new atomic power station on the south bank of the river".

Jack: "I know, I heard about it in the factory. Some of the fellows think that they may get better jobs there, and higher wages, of course".

Betty: "And the other side of the coin? Won't such an ugly plant spoil the landscape?"

Jack: "Of course it will. But it's not much different from the cooling towers and chimneys that the normal power stations in our district have".

Betty: "Well, yes. It seems that we've no choice. After all we must have more and more electric power. But why doesn't the government stick to coal and oil?"

Jack: "We already have a sufficient number of these power stations. You see, uranium and the other materials that are used for nuclear fission are cheaper fuel".

Betty: "There's a sketch here, below the text, does it make sense to you?"

Jack: "Yes, look here, this is the reactor. And in the reactor there is the combustion chamber. They put in the atomic fuel rods which contain a number of small uranium pellets. The reaction heats up the water in the boilers and they can produce steam for quite a long time".

Betty: "And how exactly does that work? Do the pellets explode?"

Jack: "Well, I'm not a physicist. It's what is called nuclear fission. A very slow chain reaction, a retarded explosion, as it were".

Betty: "But isn't all this very dangerous? I mean the radioactivity and the radiation can kill the workers in the plant. I have heard that it is stronger than X-rays".

Jack: "I think, on the whole it is quite safe. You see, the reactor is in the atomic pile – here, that's it – the gigantic concrete egg.
But I wouldn't want to be a fish in our river; it's inevitable that the temperature of the river water will rise. That will mean bad times for anglers. Another price we must pay for progress".

Betty: "Speaking of progress, if we get enough electricity from this plant, why shouldn't the Turners get a new electrical heating system for their house? That would be progress for a housewife".

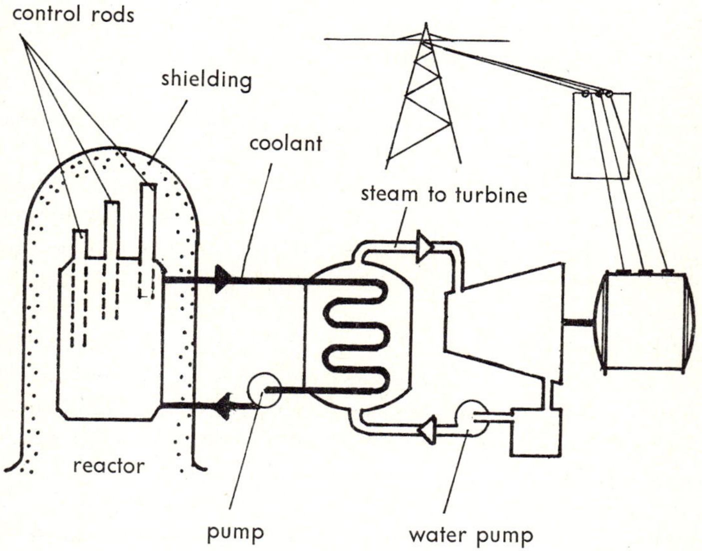

NUCLEAR REACTOR

Lesson 14B

Power Stations

Electricity is made at power stations in different parts of the country. It is made by generators. We can use water, coal, oil or uranium to make power to drive the generators. Water power is cheap, especially in mountainous regions. Water always flows downhill. It can be used to turn the wheels of water turbines which drive electric generators. These power stations are called hydro-electric-power stations.

We can find coal-fired power stations near coal-fields or where coal is cheap. The coal is put into furnaces beneath the boilers where steam is made. The steam is used to drive steam turbines which drive the generators. Instead of coal oil can be used.

Uranium is used to make atomic power in nuclear (atomic) power staions.

When electricity is made by a generator, it is about 11000 volts. It has to pass through a transformer so that it has enough power to travel long distances. Transformers can change the voltage up to 132000 volts or 275000 volts. Then the electricity is carried by cables (power lines) from pylon to pylon across the country to sub-stations. Here it is stepped down through transformers to 11000 volts again and carried through underground cables to towns, where it is transformed down in smaller sub-stations to 240 (220) volts so that we can use it in our homes.

One of the problems in a modern industrial society is pollution. Power stations need cooling towers to cool down the water after the steam has been made. Rivers can be polluted if the hot water is released directly into the rivers. The air can be polluted by the black smoke from the furnaces at power stations.

Exercises 14:

a) Answer these questions:
   1. What fuel is used at power stations?
   2. What must be done at the sub-stations before we can use electricity in our homes?
   3. Why do power stations in the mountains produce so-called clean energy?
   4. Why can't we use wind and sun to make all the energy we need?

b) Here are some answers. Can you write down the questions?
   1. These power stations are usually near a dam which has been built at the narrowest point of the valley.
   2. It's the best place, because a lot of water is needed for the boilers and cooling towers.
   3. Yes, that's right, and everybody who works inside the reactor building must wear special protective clothing and carry a Geiger-counter.
   4. No, they can't, these concrete walls are too thick.

c) Change these sentences into the passive voice:
   Example: We can use water to make electricity. (Water can be used to make .....
   1. We can find coal-fired power stations near coal-fields.
   2. We use uranium to make atomic power.
   3. We step down the voltage at sub stations.
   4. We cool down the water in cooling towers.
   5. We will pollute air and water if we are not careful.

d) Translate these sentences into German. Begin with the word – man:
   Example: Electricity is made at power stations (Man produziert Strom .....)
   1. Hydro-electric power stations are built in the mountains.
   2. Chimneys were built higher and higher.
   3. In the first power stations only coal was used.
   4. More and more power stations will be built.
   5. The power lines and dams cannot be fully protected against a catastrophe.

Lesson 15A

Getting Ready for the Party

Jack Turner: "Everything ready for the party? Mum and I will be off in a minute. And don't forget – tell your friends not to make too much noise. We don't want any more trouble with the neighbours".

Mary Turner: "Well, Dad, I'll do my best. But there's another problem – could you just have a quick look at my cassette recorder? I had some trouble with the cassette last time I used it, but I couldn't find out what was wrong with it. Please, Daddy, you're an expert, you can fix things in no time".

Jack: "All right. I'll have a quick look at it. But if it's going to take longer I can't do it now, I'm afraid".

Mary: "Thanks, Dad. If you can't get it working again, we'll use the record player. It works perfectly well with the new speakers and I've fitted a new stylus".

Jack: "That's good. I prefer our LPs (long play records). Our folksongs and waltzes are so much nicer than your tapes with all that pop music.
Now, look – there's something wrong with the lid. It won't shut properly. Perhaps we'll have to put a new spring in. If you press the lid down firmly when you are closing it after you put in the cassette it might do for tonight. If it won't stay closed you'll just have to leave it. And don't let your friends start fumbling with it."

Mary: "All right, Dad. We'll have a good time, anyway. And there's always Tom. He can sing a lot of pop songs. He usually sings in our school group".

Jack: "Well, I can imagine how the neighbours will appreciate that. At least it will be something new for them."

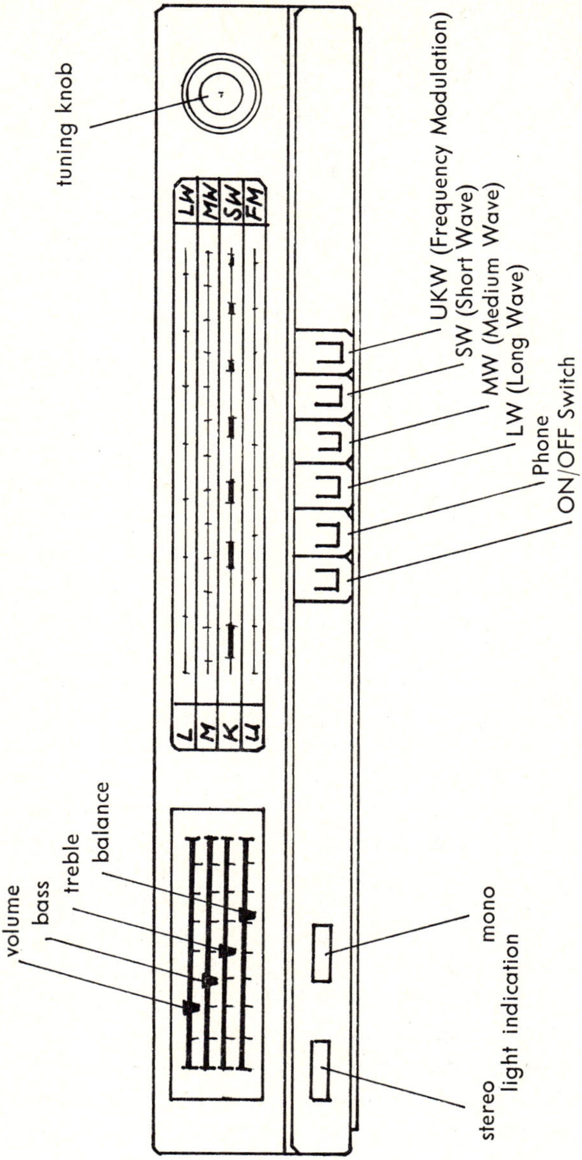
tuning knob
LW
MW
SW
FM
L
M
K
U
UKW (Frequency Modulation)
SW (Short Wave)
MW (Medium Wave)
LW (Long Wave)
Phone
ON/OFF Switch
volume
bass
treble
balance
mono
stereo
light indication

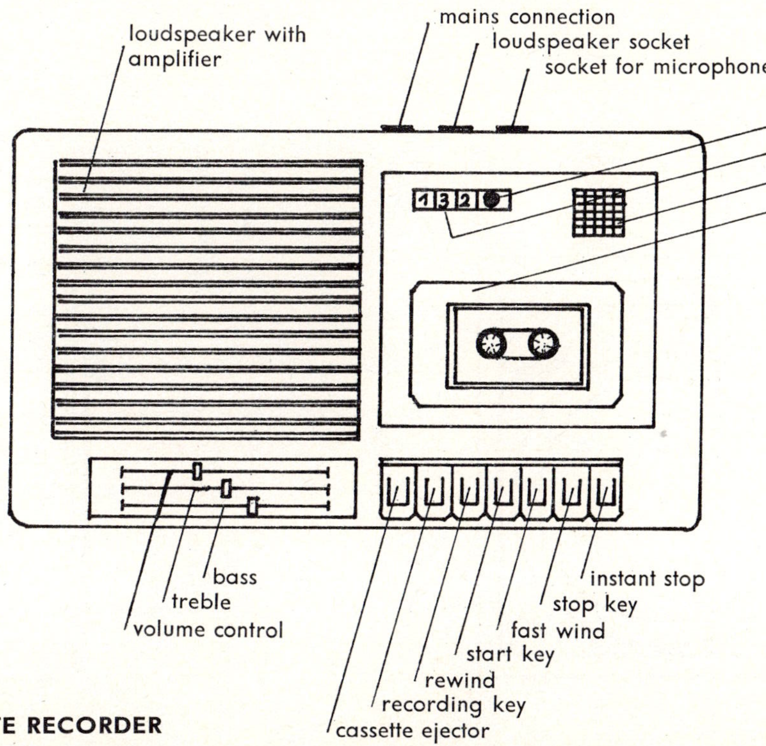

CASSETTE RECORDER

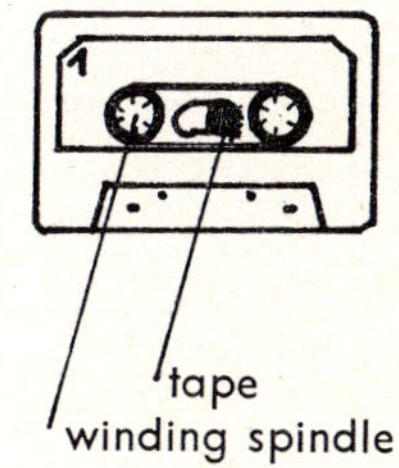

CASSETTE

RECORD PLAYER

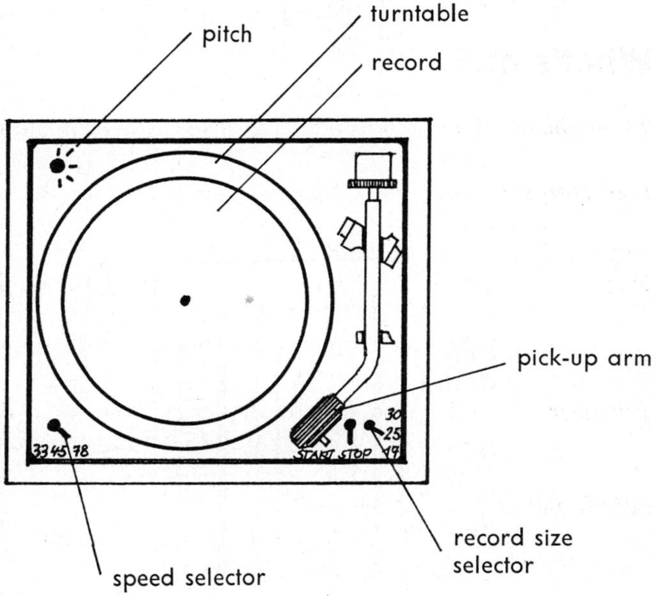

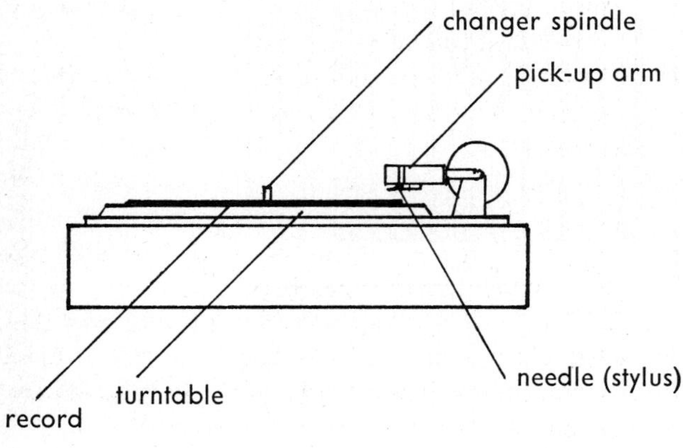

Lesson 15B

What's on?

TV engineer: "Good morning. I believe your television isn't working".

Fred Harper: "Yes, that's right. Come in. It's in the sitting room".

Engineer: "And what's the trouble?"

Fred: "Well, it was working quite well, although it was a bit noisy. Then the picture started to flicker a few times and it went off. Now we only have the sound".

Engineer: "I'll see what I can do. If it's a big job, I'll have to take it back to the workshop. If it's the aerial I can fix it right now.

(about half an hour later)

"Well, I've got your picture clear again".

Fred: "So it wasn't the tube then?"

Engineer: "No, it was just a transistor. That's not so expensive.

Fred: "And what about the noise? We seem to get it more on the second channel. Has it anything to do with the channel selector?"

Engineer: "I don't think so. It's probably just a matter of tuning. You turn this knob slightly until it improves".

Fred: "Well, thank you very much. The children will be glad to have the TV back again".

Engineer: "You'll have to adjust the brightness and contrast when you change channels".

Fred: "Well, I always do, and the children and their friends are always fumbling with the controls when they switch the set on or change to another channel".

Engineer: "I know. But one last thing which many people often forget; keep the screen clean, you'll get a better picture".

Exercises 15:

a) Compare: (use as – as; not as – as; (comparative) than

1. I prefer the LP; the sound is ..... the sound of a cassette. (good)
2. It's not a question of money. The LP is ..... the cassette. (expensive)
3. The colour on our TV is ..... the colour on this new model. (bright)
4. You can take your TV set to the workshop in the department store. It's a bit ..... at the TV service shop but you have to wait ..... there. (cheap; long)

b) Write the sentences in the passive:

Example: She recorded *the song* last year – *The song* was recorded last year.

1. He fitted *a new stylus* yesterday.
2. He always rewinds *the tape* before starting to record.
3. We will repair *the cassette* tomorrow.
4. We connected *the speakers* to the record player.
5. Look here, I depress *the start and record* keys together.
6. He plugged in the microphone.

c) Form sentences with these phrases, then answer and begin with a) yes, b) no

Example: check the tube

Have you checked the tube yet?

a) Yes, I've already checked it.

b) No, I haven't checked it yet.

1. adjust the brightness
2. plug in the aerial
3. change the valves

4. fix the channel selector
5. switch the set off
6. repair the volume control

d) Something is wrong here. Find out what it is and put in the right words:
   1. You have to rewind the tape on a record player.
   2. I had to buy a new stylus for my cassette recorder.
   3. Did you have to fit a new valve in the lid?
   4. You will have to depress the aerial and the microphone if you want to record this song.
   5. The engineer didn't have to wire the channel selector.
   6. You must keep the tuning knobs clean to get a better picture.

Hinweise zur Arbeit mit dem Wörterverzeichnis, den alphabetischen Registern, Listen und Tabellen.

Die im folgenden angegebenen Wörter behandeln technische Begriffe und Tätigkeiten und sind auf den Inhalt der Lektionen bezogen. Sie stimmen, wenn es nicht zusätzlich angegeben ist, mit den allgemeinen Bedeutungen wie sie in Anfängerlehrbüchern und einfachen Wörterbüchern gegeben werden, oft nicht überein.
Die alphabetischen Wortregister in englischer und deutscher Sprache haben deshalb zum Nachschlagen über den Wortschatz der Umgangssprache nur begrenzten Wert.
Bei der Aufstellung des Wörterverzeichnisses, der Register und Listen wurden folgende Wörterbücher benutzt, die gleichzeitig zu vertiefender Information empfohlen werden:

1) Henry Freeman, „Technisches Taschenwörterbuch, deutsch–englisch, englisch-deutsch“ 2 Bde. Max Hueber Verlag, München.
2) The English Duden – zweisprachiges Bildwörterbuch, Bibl. Institut – Dudenverlag, Mannheim
3) A. S. Hornby „Oxford Advanced Learner's Dictionary of Current English”, (New Edition), London – Oxford Univ. Press

Für die phonetische Schrift wurde “Daniel Jones, An English Pronouncing Dictionary” benutzt.
Die Abkürzung U.S. hinter einem Wort bedeutet, daß diese Bezeichnung im amerikanischen Englisch üblich ist. U.K. bedeutet “United Kingdom” (Großbritannien). Das Zeichen *R* hinter einem Wort oder einem aus mehreren Wörtern bestehendem Ausdruck bedeutet, daß es sich um eine spracheigentümliche englische Redewendung und die sinngemäße, nicht wörtliche Übertragung handelt.
Ein Stern (*) hinter einem auf r endenden Wort bedeutet, daß das r nur ausgesprochen wird, wenn ein Wort mit Vokalanlaut folgt.

Wörterverzeichnis der Lektionen

Lesson 1A

do it yourself *R*	[jɔːˈsel|f]	mach es selbst!
d.i.y. enthusiast	[inˈθjuːziæst]	Heimwerker
After his return from New York he paid us a visit	[ˈvizit]	Nach seiner Rückkehr aus New York besuchte er uns.
d.i.y. center (centre)	[ˈsent|ə*]	Heimwerkermarkt, H.-Einkaufszentrum
tools	[tuːlz]	Werkzeug
material	[məˈtiəriəl]	Material
The carpenter needs a new saw.		Der Zimmermann braucht eine neue Säge.
to paper		tapezieren
wallpaper	[ˈwɔːl.peipə*]	Tapete
to tile	[tail]	kacheln; fliesen
bookcase	[ˈbukkeis]	Bücherschrank; Regal mit Einlegeböden
shelf	[ʃel|f]	Regalbrett
The 'Do It Yourself Centre' has whatever you need.	[wɔtˈevə*]	Das ‚Do It Yourself' Zentrum hat alles was Sie brauchen.
board	[bɔːd]	Brett; Tafel
timber	[ˈtimbə*]	Bauholz
These two tables are different in size	[ˈdifrənt]	Diese zwei Küchentische sind von unterschiedlicher Größe.
size	[saiz]	Größe
type	[taip]	Typ
to choose; chose; chosen	[tʃuːz; tʃouz; tʃouzn]	aussuchen, auswählen
He chose the most expensive saw in the shop.		Er suchte sich die teuerste Säge im Laden aus.
electric	[iˈlektrik]	elektrisch
saw		Säge
to saw		sägen
set (of tools)		Satz (Werkzeug)
screwdriver	[ˈskruː.draivə*]	Schraubenzieher
bit	[bit]	Bohreinsatz (el. und Handbohrer)
chisel	[ˈtʃiz|l]	Meißel
to chisel		meißeln
rule	[ruːl]	Gliedermaßstab; Zollstock

My husband is all thumbs. *R*	[θʌmz]	Mein Man hat zwei linke Hände; er ist ungeschickt
thumb	[θʌm]	Daumen
hammer	[ˈhæmə*]	Hammer
to hammer		hämmern; einschlagen
nail	[neil]	Nagel
straight	[streit]	gerade
drill		Bohrer
to drill		bohren
to repair	[riˈpɛə*]	reparieren
repair job		Reparatur

Lesson 1B

football results	[riˈzʌlts]	Fußballergebnisse
advertisement	[ədˈvɔːtismənt]	Zeitungsanzeige; Reklame
advert	[ˈædvəːt]	Anzeige (Kurzform)
At £10 this dress is a bargain	[ˈbɑːgin]	Für £10 ist dieses Kleid spottbillig.
bargain		günstiges Angebot; Sonderangebot.
The young student is handing out leaflets to the passers-by.	[ˈliːflits]	Der junge Student verteilt Flugblätter an die Passanten.
This set of instructions is written in four languages.	[inˈstrʌkʃənz]	Diese Arbeitsanleitung ist in vier Sprachen abgefaßt.
prefabricated	[ˈpriːˈfæbrikeitid]	vorgefertigt
piece		(Bau)teil; Einzelteil; Stück
measurements	[ˈmeʒə*mənts]	Maße; Maßangaben
to cut to size	[saiz]	auf Maß (Größe) schneiden
joint	[dʒɔint]	Verbindungsstelle; Fuge; Verbindungsstück; Gelenk; Muffe
to join together	[dʒɔin]	verbinden, zusammenfügen
to mark	[mɑːk]	markieren
mark		Markierung
hole	[həul]	Loch
He painted the ceiling red.	[ˈpeintid]	Er hat die Decke rot gestrichen.

Our boat is getting a second coat of paint.	[kəut]	Unser Boot bekommt einen zweiten Anstrich.
primer	[ˈpraimə*]	Grundierung
to prime	[praim]	grundieren
undercoat	[kəut]	erster Farbanstrich
top coat		Deckanstrich; Lackierung

Lesson 2A

That was a good piece of advice!	[ədˈvais]	Das war ein guter Ratschlag!
expert	[ˈekspəːt]	Fachmann
office	[ˈɔfis]	Büro
(work) bench	[bentʃ]	(Werk)bank
workshop	[ˈwəːkʃɔp]	Werkstatt
skilful	[ˈskil|ful]	geschickt
mechanic	[miˈkænik]	Mechaniker
file	[fail]	hier: Feile (Werkzeug)
to file		feilen (Material)
to be surprised	[səˈpraizd]	überrascht sein
to suggest	[səˈdʒest]	vorschlagen
He set up a workshop in the garage		Er hat sich eine Werkstatt in der Garage eingerichtet.
shed	[ʃed]	Schuppen
useful	[ˈjuːs|ful]	nützlich
hint	[hint]	Hinweis; Tip
basic equipment	[ˈbeisik iˈkwipmənt]	Grundausrüstung; -ausstattung
We have to cut down on our expenses.	[iksˈpensiz]	Wir müssen unsere Ausgaben einschränken.
housekeeping money		Haushaltsgeld
on the one hand *R*		einerseits
on the other hand *R*		andererseits
She saved a lot of money last year.		Sie hat letztes Jahr viel Geld gespart.
workman (skilled)	[ˈwəːkmən]	Facharbeiter
bill		Rechnung

Lesson 2B

to check	[tʃek]	durchgehen (Liste); überprüfen
several	[ˈsevr|əl]	mehrere

pincers (pair of p.)	[ˈpinsəz]	Kneifzange
spanner	[ˈspænə*]	Schraubenschlüssel
tool box	[ˈtu:l bɔks]	Werkzeugkasten
lawn mower	[ˈlɔ:n.məuə*]	Rasenmäher
to tighten	[ˈtait|n]	anziehen (Schraube; Mutter)
to loosen	[ˈlu:s|n]	lockern; lösen
loose	[lu:s]	locker; lose
to lose, lost, lost	[lu:z, lɔst]	verlieren
nut	[nʌt]	Mutter
bolt	[bəult]	Bolzen, große Schraube mit Gewinde
What about this wall? It needs a new coat of paint.		Was ist mit dieser Wand? Sie braucht einen neuen Anstrich.
wood screw	[ˈwudskru:]	Holzschraube
wing screw	[wiŋ]	Flügelschraube
wing nut		Flügelmutter
rawl plug	[rɔ:l plʌg]	Dübel, Mauerdübel
spacer	[ˈspeisə*]	Unterlegscheibe
thread	[θred]	Gewinde; Faden
head		Kopf (Schraube; Bolzen)
square	[skwɛə*]	viereckig; Viereck
hexagonal	[hekˈsægən|l]	sechseckig
local hardware shop	[ˈləuk|əl ˈhɑ:d-wɛə* ʃɔp]	örtliche Eisenwarenhandlung
by the way *R*		übrigens, im übrigen
pliers (pair of combination pliers)	[ˈplaiəz]	Kombizange
wire	[ˈwaiə*]	Draht
handsaw		kleine Handsäge, Fuchsschwanz
fretsaw	[ˈfret|sɔ:]	Laubsäge
frame-saw	[ˈfreim|sɔ:]	Bügelsäge, Rahmensäge
hacksaw	[ˈhæksɔ:]	Eisensäge
iron	[ˈaiən]	Eisen
hinges	[ˈhindʒiz]	Scharniere; Türangeln
next item	[ˈaitəm]	nächster Punkt (Liste; Tagesordnung)
gimlet	[ˈgimlit]	Nagelbohrer
wrench	[rentʃ]	(verstellbarer) Schraubenschlüssel
vice	[vais]	Schraubstock
The clock was fast. He adjusted it.	[əˈdʒʌs|tid]	Die Uhr ging vor. Er hat sie richtig eingestellt.

This screw is too big. It doesn't fit.		Diese Schraube ist zu groß. Sie paßt nicht.
cap nut		Hutmutter
stop nut		Verschlußmutter
lock nut		Kontermutter
The wheel came off easily.		Das Rad ging leicht ab.
clerk	[klɑːk]	Büroangestellter
plumber	[plʌmə*]	Installateur (Wasser; Gas)
to be nuts *R*		verrückt sein
to have a screw loose *R*		nicht normal sein, eine Schraube locker haben
spoilsport	[ˈspɔilspɔːt]	Spielverderber
plane	[plein]	hier: Hobel
to plane		hobeln
woodwork		Holzarbeit

Lesson 3A

factory	[ˈfæktər|i]	Fabrik
later than usual	[ˈjuː|ʒuəl]	später als gewöhnlich
Jack Turner is a good friend of mine, and he lives next door.		Jack Turner ist ein guter Freund von mir, und er wohnt nebenan.
car	[kɑː*]	Auto
He has to take his car to the garage.	[ˈgærɑːʒ]	Er muß sein Auto zur Werkstatt bringen.
service station, filling station	[ˈsəːvis ˈsteiʃ|ən] [ˈfiliŋ ˈsteiʃ|ən]	Tankstelle
engine	[ˈendʒin]	Motor
Are you tired, Jane? As a matter of fact I am. *R*		Bist du müde, Jane? Eigentlich ja.
machine	[məˈʃiːn]	Maschine
to promise	[ˈprɔmis]	versprechen
operator	[ˈɔpəreitə*]	Bediener (Maschine); Telefonistin
to operate	[ˈɔpəreit]	bedienen (Maschine; Gerät)
lathe	[leið]	Drehmaschine, Drehbank
funny	[ˈfʌn|i]	komisch; merkwürdig; spaßig
harp	[hɑːp]	Harfe
idea	[aiˈdiə]	Idee

to think something over		etwas bedenken; überlegen
Anyway, I have to go home now.		Jedenfalls muß ich jetzt nach Hause.
anyway *R*		jedenfalls; sowieso, wie dem auch sei

Lesson 3B

function	[ˈfʌŋkʃ|ən]	Funktion
to put in		hier: einspannen
piece of material (workpiece)	[məˈtiəriəl]	Werkstück
turning tool		Drehmeißel
to start		anlassen
to regulate	[ˈregjuleit]	regulieren
revolutions (revs.)	[ˌrevəˈluːʃənz]	Umdrehungen
to rotate	[rəuˈteit]	sich drehen; rotieren
speed	[spiːd]	Geschwindigkeit
process	[ˈprəuses]	bearbeiten; verarbeiten
in different ways		auf verschiedene Weise
straight-turning	[streit]	Langdrehen
cylindrical	[siˈlindrikəl]	zylindrisch
to face	[feis]	plandrehen (stirndrehen)
to form-turn	[ˈfɔːmtəːn]	formdrehen; Profildrehen
profile	[ˈprəufail]	Profil
turret lathe	[ˈtʌrit leið]	Revolverdrehmaschine
operation	[ˌɔpəˈreiʃən]	Arbeitsvorgang
hole	[həul]	Loch
round bar steel	[ˈraund ˌbɑː stiːl]	Rundstahl
boring tool	[ˈbɔːriŋ tuːl]	Bohrmeißel
to bore	[bɔː*]	maschinell bohren
to turn on/off		an-; abstellen
to pull a switch	[switʃ]	Schalter betätigen
to stop		abstellen; anhalten
just	[dʒʌst]	bloß, einfach
to press	[pres]	drücken
to push in		reindrücken
button	[ˈbʌtən]	Knopf
knob	[nɔb]	Drehknopf
to push up		hochschieben, -drücken
lever	[ˈliːv|ə*]	Hebel
It takes time to become a good mechanic. *R*		Es braucht seine Zeit, bis man ein guter Mechaniker wird.
experience	[iksˈpiəriəns]	Erfahrung

experienced	[iks'piəriənst]	erfahren
machinist	[mə'ʃi:nist]	Maschinist
to imagine	[i'mædʒin]	sich etwas vorstellen
planer (planing machine)	['pleinə*]	Langhobelmaschine
shaper (shaping machine)	['ʃeip|ə*]	Waagerechtstoßmaschine (Umgangssprache Kurzhobler)
to plane	[plein]	langhobeln
to shape	[ʃeip]	stoßen (kurzhobeln)
tool		hier: Meißel für Maschinen
special	['speʃ|əl]	extra; besonders
beginner	[bi|'ginə*]	Anfänger
operation	[.ɔpə'reiʃən]	Arbeitsvorgang
kind of		Art
milling machine		Fräse
to mill		fräsen
groove; grooves (pl.)	[gru:v]	Nut; Rille; Rinne
to slab-mill	[slæb]	walzfräsen
spindle	['spind|l]	Spindel (Bohrfräsmaschine)
plain-milling-cutter	['plein miliŋ 'kʌtə*]	Walzenfräser (Meißel)
to set (machine)		einrichten
shell-end-milling	['ʃel-end-'miliŋ]	stirnfräsen
to fix		einsetzen; anbringen; befestigen (in Ordnung bringen)
milling cutter		Fräser
automatic press	[.ɔ:tə'mætik pres]	automatische Presse
punching machine	['pʌntʃiŋ]	Stanze
to punch	[pʌntʃ]	stanzen, lochen
metal	['metl]	Metall

Lesson 3C

operating instruction	[in'strʌkʃən]	Bedienungsanleitung
directions for use	[di'rekʃənz]	Gebrauchsanweisung
A good driver always keeps his eyes on the road.		Ein guter Fahrer paßt im Straßenverkehr immer auf.
to keep an eye on something, somebody		jemanden, etwas im Auge behalten
regular	['regjulə*]	hier: regelmäßig
interval	['intəvəl]	Zeitabstand

to grease; grease	[gri:s]	abschmieren; Schmierfett
to lubricate	[ˈlu:brikeit]	abschmieren; ölen
lubricant	[ˈlu:brikənt]	Schmieröl
spare parts	[spɛə* pɑts]	Ersatzteile
to be handy *R*	[ˈhændi]	griffbereit sein
to replace	[riˈpleis]	ersetzen
to be worn		abgenutzt sein; verschlissen;
to wear, wore, worn	[wɛə*]	sich abnutzen
to be broken		kaputt sein;
to break, broke, broken		kaputt gehen
to assemble	[əˈsemb|l]	zusammensetzen
to disassemble	[ˈdisəsembl]	auseinandernehmen
to reassemble	[ˈri:əsembl]	wieder zusammensetzen
complicated	[ˈkɔmplikeitid]	kompliziert
to leave, left, left		hier: überlassen (eine Arbeit)
fitter	[ˈfitə*]	Monteur; Maschinenbauschlosser
vernier caliper	[ˈvə:niə ˈkælipə*]	Schieblehre; Meßschieber

Lesson 4A

to install	[inˈstɔ:l]	installieren
hot water geyser	[ˈgaizə*]	Heißwassergerät; Durchlauferhitzer
to warn	[wɔ:n]	warnen
I spoke to my boss about the problem just the other day. *R*		Ich habe mich neulich mit meinem Chef über dieses Problem unterhalten.
joint	[dʒɔint]	hier: Muffe
pipe		hier: Rohr
In the end he gave in. *R*		Zum Schluß gab er nach.
to put something right *R*		etwas in Ordnung bringen
washer	[ˈwɔʃə*]	Dichtungsring
tap	[tæp]	Wasserhahn
stop cock	[kɔk]	Absperrhahn
mains	[meinz]	Hauptleitung (Strom; Wasser)
central heating	[ˈsentr|əl-ˈhi:tiŋ]	Zentralheizung
hot water supply	[səˈpl|ai]	Heißwasseranlage
caretaker	[ˈkɛə.teikə*]	Hausmeister
fault	[fɔ:lt]	Defekt; Fehler
leak	[li:k]	Leck; Riß

estate car; station wagon U.S.	[is'teitkɑ:*] ['steiʃən ˌwægən]	Kombiwagen
welding gear	['weldiŋ giə*]	Schweißgerät
soldering gear		Lötgerät
to weld	[weld]	schweißen
to solder	['sɔ:ldə*]	löten
welder	['weldə*]	Schweißer
solderer	['sɔ:ldərə*]	Löter
soldering iron	['aiən]	Lötkolben
welding shop		Schweißerei
welding torch	[tɔ:tʃ]	Schweißbrenner
welding rod	[rɔd]	Schweißstab
soft	[sɔft]	weich
steel plate	['sti:l 'pleit]	Stahlplatte
oxy-acetylene	['ɔksiə'setili:n]	Sauerstoff-Azetylen
cylinder	'silində*]	Flasche
to protect from	[prə'tekt]	schützen vor
protective clothing	[prə'tektiv]	Schutzkleidung
spark	[spɑ:k]	Funken
to glare	[glɛə*]	gleißen; hell strahlen
handshield	['hændʃi:ld]	Schweißschirm, -schutz
safety goggles	['seifti 'gɔg|lz]	Schutzbrille
helmet	['helmit]	Schutzhelm

Lesson 4B

steel plant	[plɑ:nt]	Stahlwerk
apprentice	[ə'prentis]	Lehrling
excited	[ik'saitid]	aufgeregt
engineer	[ˌendʒi'niə*]	Ingenieur
The foreman took Henry round the steel mill.	['fɔ:mən]	Der Vorarbeiter führte Henry in dem Stahlwerk herum.
locksmith	['lɔksmiθ]	Schlosser
lock		Schloß, Türschloß
to lock		zuschließen
to unlock		aufschließen
canteen	[kæn'ti:n]	Kantine
The doctor put me in the picture about my health. *R*		Der Arzt hat mich über meine Gesundheit ins Bild gesetzt.
At first glance the job seemed to be hard.	[glɑ:ns]	Auf den ersten Blick schien die Arbeit schwer zu sein.

routine	[ru:ˈti:n]	Routine, Gewohnheit
tank	[tæŋk]	Kessel, Tank
boiler	[bɔilə*]	Heizkessel
pipe system	[ˈpaip sistim]	Rohrleitungsanlage
pipeline	[ˈpaip-lain]	Rohrleitung (Fernleitung)
important	[imˈpɔ:tən|t]	wichtig
A foreman is responsible for his workers.	[risˈpɔnsəb|l]	Ein Vorarbeiter ist für seine Arbeiter verantwortlich.
She is a good secretary. You can rely on her.	[riˈl|ai]	Sie ist eine gute Sekretärin. Sie können sich auf sie verlassen.
reliable	[riˈlaiəb|l]	zuverlässig
indicator	[ˈindikeitə*]	Anzeigegerät
to indicate	[ˈindikeit]	anzeigen
thermometer	[θəˈmɔmitə*]	Thermometer
gauge	[geidʒ]	Meßgerät
scale	[skeil]	Skala
chap	[tʃæp]	Bursche
to explain	[iksˈplein]	erklären
needle	[ˈni:dl]	Nadel
He saw at a glance that something was wrong with the boiler. *R*	[glɑ:ns]	Beim ersten Blick sah er, daß etwas mit dem Boiler nicht stimmte.
temperature	[ˈtempritʃə*]	Temperatur
pressure	[ˈpreʃə*]	Druck
constant	[ˈkɔnstənt]	konstant; gleichbleibend
control system	[kənˈtrəul ˈsistim]	Steuerungsanlage
develop an instinct	[diˈveləp; ˈinstiŋkt]	Gefühl für etwas entwickeln
prospects	[ˈprɔspekts]	Zukunftsaussichten
On the whole I'm satisfied with my job. *R*	[houl] [ˈsætis|faid]	Im großen und ganzen bin ich mit meiner Arbeit zufrieden.
coal mine	[ˈkəulmain]	Kohlenbergwerk; Zeche
chemical plant	[ˈkemikəl ˌplɑ:nt]	Chemiewerk
oil corporation	[ˈɔil ˌkɔ:pəˈreiʃən]	Ölgesellschaft
drilling rig	[rig]	Bohrplattform; -insel
terribly	[ˈterəb|li]	furchtbar

Lesson 5A

exterior (n) (adj.)	[eksˈtiəriə*]	das Äußere, äußerlich
motor-car	[ˈməutəkɑ:*]	Auto; Kraftwagen

roof	[ru:f]	Dach
body		Karosserie
chassis	[ˈʃæsi]	Fahrgestell
windscreen	[ˈwindskri:n]	Windschutzscheibe
w.-shield (U.S)	[ˈwindʃi:ld]	
windscreen wiper	[waipə*]	Scheibenwischer
heated rear window	[ˈhi:tid riə*]	heizbare Heckscheibe; Rückfenster
wing mirror	[ˈwiŋ ˈmirə*]	Außenrückspiegel
rear-view mirror	[ˈriə vju: ˈmirə*]	Rückblickspiegel
door handle	[ˈhænd|l]	Türgriff
door lock	[lɔk]	Schloß
bonnet/hood (U.S.)	[ˈbɔnit/hud]	Motorhaube
aerial	[ˈɛəriəl]	Antenne
boot	[bu:t, trʌŋk]	Kofferraum
trunk (U.S.)		
boot lid		Kofferraumdeckel
boot lock		Kofferraumschloß
mudguard/fender (U.S.)	[ˈmʌdgɑ:d] [ˈfendə*]	Kotflügel
radiator grill	[ˈreidieitə* gril]	Kühlergrill; -gitter
number plate		Nummernschild
licence number	[ˈlaisəns]	Zulassungsnummer
headlights		Scheinwerfer
dipped beam	[ˈdipt bi:m]	Abblendlicht
full beam		Fernlicht
parking light		Standlicht
fog lights		Nebelleuchten
rear fog lights	[ˈriə]	Nebelschlußleuchte
rear lights		Rückleuchten; Rücklichter
brake lights	[breik]	Bremslichter
reversing lights	[riˈvə:siŋ]	Rückfahrscheinwerfer
trafficator/indicator	[ˈindikeitə*]	Blinker; Fahrtrichtungsanzeiger
bumper	[ˈbʌmpə*]	Stoßstange
horn	[hɔ:n]	Hupe
wheel		Rad
hub cap	[hʌb]	Radkappe
rim		Felge
tyre, tire (U.S.)	[ˈtaiə*]	Reifen
tubeless	[ˈtju:blis]	schlauchlos
valve	[vælv]	Ventil
to inflate	[inˈfleit]	aufpumpen
valve cap		Ventilkappe; -verschluß
exhaust pipe	[igˈzɔ:st paip]	Auspuffrohr

silencer	['sailənsə*]	Auspufftopf
petrol cap	['petr|əl]	Tankklappe; -verschluß
dent		Beule; Delle

Lesson 5B

interior	[in'tiəriə*]	das Innere; innerlich
dashboard	['dæʃbɔ:d]	Armaturenbrett
speedometer	[spi'dɔmitə*]	Tachometer
odometer	[əu'dɔmitə*]	Kilometerzähler
fuel gauge	['fjuəl ˌgeidʒ]	Kraftstoffanzeiger
temperature gauge	['tempritʃə]	Temperaturanzeiger
oil pressure gauge	['preʃə*]	Öldruckmsser
warning lights (6+7)		Kontrolleuchten
ignition light (generator warning light)	[ig'niʃən] ['dʒenəreitə] ['wɔniŋ]	Lichtmaschinenanzeiger
dipswitch	['dipswitʃ]	Abblendlichtschalter
ventilation control lever	[ˌventi'leiʃən] [kən'trəul]	Lüftungsregulierungshebel
fresh air vents	[vents]	Lüftungsschlitze
heater switch	['hi:tə*]	Heizungsschalterknopf
fan	[fæn]	Gebläse; Ventilator
steering wheel	['stiəriŋwi:l]	Lenkrad
adjusting knob (clock)		Stellknopf; Regulierungsknopf
radio	['reidiəu]	Radio
trafficator/indicator lever	['træfikeitə*/ 'indikeitə*] ['li:və*]	Blinkerhebel
warning flasher	['hæzəd]	Warnblinkleuchte
hazard flasher	['flæʃə*]	Lichthupe
manual choke	['mænjuəl tʃəuk]	Starterklappe
inside rear-view mirror	['riə vju: 'mirə*]	Innenrückspiegel
bonnet catch release	[ri'li:s]	Hebel zur Entriegelung der Motorhaube
petrol cap release	['petrəl-ri'li:s]	Hebel zur Entriegelung der Tankklappe
ashtray	['æʃtrei]	Aschenbecher
glove compartment	[glʌv kəm'pɑ:tmənt]	Handschuhfach
ignition switch	[ig'niʃən]	Zündschloß
ignition key	[ki:]	Zündschlüssel
gear lever	[giə*]	Schalthebel; Ganghebel
automatic transmission	[trænz'miʃən]	Getriebeautomatik

accelerator (gas) pedal	[əkˈseləreitə* gæs ˈped|l]	Gaspedal
to accelerate	[əkˈseləreit]	beschleunigen; Gas geben
brake pedal		Bremspedal
to brake		bremsen
clutch pedal	[klʌtʃ]	Kupplungspedal
handbrake		Handbremse
to drive, drove, driven		fahren
driver's seat	[ˈdraivəz siːt]	Fahrersitz
passenger seat	[ˈpæsindʒə*]	Beifahrersitz
window handle		Fensterkurbel
arm rest	[rest]	Armstütze
head rest		Kopfstütze
seat belt	[ˈsiːt belt]	Gurt
seat belt buckle	[ˈbʌk|l]	Gurtverriegelung

Lesson 6A

neutral (neutral gear)	[ˈnjuːtr|əl]	Leerlauf
clockwise	[ˈklɔk|waiz]	im Uhrzeigersinn; in Uhrzeigerrichtung
to start		anlassen; anspringen (Motor)
starter	[ˈstɑːtə*]	Anlasser
to run smoothly	[ˈsmuːðli]	rundlaufen; normal laufen (Motor)
to fasten	[ˈfɑːs|n]	einhaken; befestigen
fasten your seat belt		schnallen Sie sich an
to depress	[diˈpres]	treten; durchteten
first (bottom) gear	[ˈbɔtəm]	erster Gang
reverse gear	[riˈvəːs giə*]	Rückwärtsgang
to reverse		zurücksetzen (Auto)
to release the clutch	[riˈliːs]	Kupplung kommen lassen
to signal	[ˈsign|l]	anzeigen; Signal-Zeichen geben
to move off		losfahren
gently	[ˈdʒent|li]	sachte; sanft
to guide	[gaid]	einweisen; einwinken (Auto); führen
to gather speed	[ˈgæð|ə* spiːd]	Fahrt aufnehmen; schneller werden
to change up, down		in einen höheren Gang schalten; in einen niedrigeren Gang schalten

oil level	[ˈɔil ˈlev|l]	Ölstand
to overtake		überholen
to slow down		Geschwindigkeit verringern; langsamer fahren
level	[ˈlevl]	Stand; Niveau

Lesson 6B

trouble	[ˈtrʌb|l]	Ärger; Sorgen
We've had nothing but trouble with this new car.		Wir haben nichts als Ärger mit diesem neuen Auto gehabt.
fuse	[fju:z]	Sicherung
enough	[iˈnʌf]	genügend; genug
to use up		aufbrauchen; verbrauchen
to fix		hier: in Ordnung bringen; reparieren
dangerous	[ˈdeindʒrəs]	gefährlich
absolutely	[ˈæbsəlu:tli]	völlig
how right you are *R*		wie wahr!; wie recht du hast!
fine		Geldstrafe
speeding	[ˈspi:diŋ]	zu schnelles Fahren; Geschwindigkeitsüberschreitung
bulb	[bʌlb]	Glühbirne
I can't go to the cinema tonight. I've run out of money. *R*		Ich kann heute abend nicht ins Kino gehen. Mir ist das Geld ausgegangen.
blimey *R*	[ˈblaimi]	etwa: Menschenskind!
to suppose	[səˈpəuz]	vermuten; nehmen
exactly	[igˈzækt|li]	genau so
quarter	[ˈkwɔ:tə*]	Viertel
to ride		fahren (Rad, Moped, Motorrad)

Lesson 7A

second-hand car		Gebraucht-(Wagen etc.)
car dealer	[ˈdi:lə*]	Autohändler
reconditioned	[ˈri:kənˈdiʃ|ənd]	generalüberholt
guarantee	[ˌgærənˈti:]	Garantie
customer	[ˈkʌstəmə*]	Kunde

consumption	[kən'sʌmpʃən]	Verbrauch
to consume	[kən'sju:m]	verbrauchen
fuel	['fjuəl]	Kraftstoff; Treibstoff; Brennstoff
gallon	['gælən]	etwa 4,5 Liter (Gallone)
traffic	['træfik]	Verkehr
maintenance	['meintənəns]	Wartung; Instandhaltung
my car needs a service		mein Auto muß zur Inspektion
to service	['sə:vis]	warten; pflegen (Auto; Geräte)
extras	['ekstrəz]	Extras; Zusatzausstattung
test drive		Probefahrt
steering	['stiəriŋ]	Lenkung
a bit slack	[slæk]	etwas Spiel haben; locker gehen
stiff		schwer gehen; steif (Lengung)
perfect running order	['pə:fikt - 'ɔ:də*]	absolut fahrbereit

Lesson 7B

to change	[tʃeindʒ]	auswechseln; wechseln
to be lucky *R*		Glück haben
This is the first time that I've ever been to New York. *R*		Das ist das erste Mal, daß ich New York besuche.
puncture	['pʌŋktʃ|ə*]	Reifenpanne
wheel spanner	[wi:l 'spænə*]	Kreuzschlüssel
car jack	[dʒæk]	Wagenheber
to jack up		hochpumpen, -heben
spare wheel	['spɛə* wi:l]	Reserverad
crosswise	['krɔswaiz]	über Kreuz

Lesson 8A

motorist	['məutərist]	Autofahrer
I wonder whether I might speak to the manager. *R*	['wʌnd/ə*]	Könnte (dürfte) ich vielleicht mit dem Geschäftsführer sprechen?
At first the mechanic was not quite sure what was wrong with the car.	[kwait]	Zuerst war der Mechaniker nicht ganz sicher, was an dem Auto nicht stimmte.

flat (battery), (tyre)		leer; schwach (Autobatterie); flach; platt (Reifen)
The new secretary has a lot of work to do, but she is getting on fine.		Die neue Sekretärin hat viel zu tun, aber sie kommt mit der Arbeit gut zurecht.
finished	[ˈfiniʃt]	fertig; erledigt
sparking plugs	[plʌgz]	Zündkerzen
contact breaker points	[ˈkɔntækt ˈbreikə*]	Unterbrecherkontake
timing	[ˈtimiŋ]	Zündzeitpunkt
carburettor	[ˈkɑːbjuret|ə*]	Vergaser
to charge (battery)	[tʃɑːdʒ]	aufladen; beladen; (Batterie);
to discharge	[ˈdistʃɑːdʒ]	entladen (Batterie)
to recharge	[ˈriːtʃɑːdʒ]	wiederaufladen
topped up	[tɔpt]	aufgefüllt
as well as *R*		ebenso wie; sowie auch und außerdem noch
not at all *R*		keine Ursache; überhaupt nicht
inside	[ˈinˈsaid]	drin
attendant	[əˈtendənt]	hier: Tankstellenwärter; Wärter; Diensthabender
receipt	[riˈsiːt]	Quittung
until	[ənˈtil]	bis

Lesson 8B

driving licence	[ˈlaisəns]	Führerschein
congratulation	[kən.grætjuˈleiʃən]	Glückwunsch
to congratulate	[kənˈgrætjuleit]	gratulieren
John passed his driving test yesterday.		John hat gestern die Fahrprüfung bestanden.
driving test		Fahrprüfung
brand-new	[brænd]	nagelneu; brandneu
to take a test		Prüfung ablegen
difficult	[ˈdifikəlt]	schwierig
to get used to	[ˈjuːstə]	sich gewöhnen an
heavy traffic		dichter Verkehr
“Don’t worry,” he said. “Everything will be okay!”	[ˈwʌr|i]	„Mach dir keine Sorgen,“ sagte er. „Alles wird gut gehen.“

to react	[ri(:)ˈækt]	reagieren
instinctively	[inˈstiŋktivli]	instinktiv; gefühlsmäßig
rush hour	[ˈrʌʃ.auə*]	Spitzenverkehrszeit; Stoßzeit
reckless	[ˈreklis]	unbesonnen; leichtfertig
practical hints	[ˈpræktik|əl]	praktische Tips
statistics	[stəkˈtistiks]	statistische Angaben
He drove too fast and caused an accident.	[ˈæksidənt]	Er fuhr zu schnell und verursachte einen Unfall.
road junction	[ˈdʒʌŋkʃən]	Straßenkreuzung
cautiously	[ˈkɔːʃəsli]	vorsichtig
to watch out		aufpassen (Verkehr)
to give way		Vorfahrt lassen
right of way		Vorfahrtsrecht
pedestrian crossing	[piˈdestriən]	Fußgängerübergang
bend		Kurve; Biegung
to approach	[əˈprəutʃ]	sich nähern
brow of a hill	[brau]	Hügelkuppe
to sound	[saund]	hier: sich anhören; klingen
highway code	[ˈhaiwei ˈkəud]	etwa: Straßenverkehrsordnung
common sense	[ˈkɔmən sens]	gesunder Menschenverstand
to start off		losfahren
elderly	[ˈeldəl|i]	älter
ever		jemals
a matter of time *R*		eine Frage der Zeit
traffic signs	[sainz]	Verkehrszeichen
to stall (engine)	[stɔːl]	abwürgen (Motor)

Lesson 9A

motorway	[ˈməutəwei]	Autobahn
highway	[ˈhaiwei]	Autostraße; Straße 1. Ordnung; 2. Fernverkehrsstraße
trunk road	[trʌŋk]	Bundesstraße
confusing	[kənˈfjuːziŋ]	verwirrend
What did the teacher just say?	[dʒʌst]	Was hat der Lehrer eben gesagt?
speed limit	[ˈlimit]	Geschwindigkeitsbegrenzung
roadworks		Straßenbauarbeiten

surface	[ˈsəːfis]	Fahrbahndecke; Oberfläche
resurfacing	[ˈriːˈsəːfisiŋ]	Erneuerung der Fahrbahndecke
official	[əˈfiʃ|əl]	amtlich
recommendation	[ˌrekəmenˈdeiʃən]	Empfehlung
to recommend	[ˌrekəˈmend]	empfehlen
to exceed	[ikˈsiːd]	überschreiten (Geschwindigkeit)
m.p.h. (miles per hour)		Meilen (1609 m) pro Stunde
lane		Fahrspur; Fahrstreifen
hard shoulder	[ˈʃouldə*]	betonierter Seitenstreifen; Standspur
narrow	[ˈnær|əu]	schmal; eng
patrol car	[pəˈtrəul]	Streifenwagen
in case		falls
breakdown		Panne
expensive	[iksˈpensiv]	teuer
to tow	[təu]	abschleppen
so		also; deshalb
except for	[ikˈsept]	außer
helicopter	[ˈhelikɔptə*]	Hubschrauber
traffic jam	[dʒæm]	Verkehrsstau

Lesson 9B

carriageway	[ˈkæridʒwei]	Fahrbahn (Autobahnseite)
direction	[diˈrekʃən]	Richtung
to keep apart	[əˈpɑːt]	auseinanderhalten; trennen
access point	[ˈækses]	Autobahnauffahrt
exit (motorway)	[ˈegzit] [ˈeksit]	Autobahnausfahrt; Ausgang
lorry	[ˈlɔr|i]	Lastkraftwagen
trailer	[treilə*]	Anhänger
long vehicle	[ˈviːikl]	langes Fahrzeug
hilly	[ˈhili]	hügelig
region	[ˈriːdʒən]	Gebiet; Region; Gegend
petrol	[ˈpetr|əl]	Benzin
to stay the night		übernachten
parking area/car park	[ˈɛəriə]	Parkplatz
lay-by		(Haltestreifen); Halteplatz

dreadful	[ˈdred|ful]	schrecklich
frequent	[ˈfriːkwənt]	häufig
cause	[kɔːz]	Ursache
close	[kləus]	dicht; nahe
wet		naß
to fall asleep		einschlafen

Lesson 10A

combustion engine	[kəmˈbʌstʃən]	Verbrennungsmotor
combustion chamber	[ˈtʃeimbə*]	Brennkammer; Verbrennungsraum
four stroke engine	[strəuk]	Viertaktmotor
coil	[kɔil]	Zündspule
distributor head	[disˈtribjutə*]	Verteilerkopf
inlet valve	[ˈinlet]	Einlaßventil
outlet	[ˈaut-let]	Austritt; Auslaß
piston	[ˈpistən]	Kolben
con rod (connecting rod)	[rɔd]	Pleuelstange
crankshaft	[ˈkræŋkʃɑːft]	Kurbelwelle
gear	[giə*]	Getriebe
exhaust (stroke)	[igˈzɔːst]	Auspuff; Ausstoßtakt
induction stroke	[ˌinˈdʌkʃən]	Ansaughub(-takt)
explosion	[iksˈpləuʒən]	Explosion
explosive	[iksˈpləusiv]	explosiv
to draw, drew, drawn		ziehen (ansaugen)
compression	[kəmˈpreʃən]	Verdichtung
to compress	[kəmˈpres]	zusammendrücken
to close	[kləuz]	schließen
to ignite	[igˈnait]	zünden

Lesson 10B

car assembly plant	[plɑːnt]	Automobilwerk
personnel manager	[ˌpəːsəˈnel ˈmænidʒə*]	Personalchef
term	[təːm]	Semester; Abschnitt
wages	[ˈweidʒiz]	Lohn
to demand	[diˈmɑːnd]	fordern
perseverance	[ˌpəːsiˈviərəns]	Ausdauer
assembly line	[əˈsembli lain]	Fließband; Montageband
dull	[dʌl]	langweilig
main line	[mein lain]	Hauptfließband

power wrench	[ˈpauə*rentʃ]	Preßluftschraubenschlüssel
hoist	[hɔist]	Kran; Hebevorrichtung
to hoist	[hɔist]	hochziehen
to keep up with *R*		Schritt halten mit
spot welding	[spɔt]	Punktschweißen
pace	[peis]	hier: Tempo; Bewegung
"You'd better take your car to a good garage." *R*		„Sie sollten lieber Ihr Auto zu einer guten Werkstatt bringen."
to report (to)	[riˈpɔːt]	(sich) melden bei
shift	[ʃift]	Schicht

Lesson 11A

possible	[ˈpɔsib|l]	möglich
to renovate	[ˈrenəuveit]	renovieren; erneuern
"Now that you live in Liverpool, I hardly ever see you." *R*		„Jetzt wo du in Liverpool wohnst, sehe ich dich kaum."
architect	[ˈɑːkitekt]	Architekt
My wife agrees with the architect on this point.	[əˈgriːz]	Meine Frau stimmt mit dem Architekten in diesem Punkt überein.
wall socket/socket	[ˈsɔkit]	Wandsteckdose/Fassung (f. Glühbirne)
at least	[liːst]	mindestens; wenigstens
watt	[wɔt]	Watt
fluorescent light	[fluəˈresnt]	Neon-Leuchtröhre
suggestion	[səˈdʒestʃən]	Vorschlag
to suggest	[səˈdʒest]	vorschlagen
special	[ˈspeʃ|əl]	extra; besonders; speziell
ceiling	[ˈsiːliŋ]	Zimmerdecke
electric appliance	[iˈlektrik əˈplaiəns]	elektrisches Gerät
egg boiler	[ˈbɔilə*]	Eierkocher
to use	[juːz]	benutzen
dishwasher	[ˈdiʃwɔʃə*]	Geschirrspülautomat
fridge (refrigerator)	[fridʒ]	Kühlschrank
deepfreezer	[ˈdiːpˈfriːzə*]	Tiefkühltruhe
cooker	[ˈkukə*]	Elektroherd
to check		hier: noch einmal durchsprechen, beraten
to overload	[ˈəuvəˈləud]	überladen; überlasten
circuit	[ˈsəːkit]	Stromkreis

distribution box	[ˌdistriˈbjuːʃən]	Verteilerdose
technical	[ˈteknik|əl]	technisch
details	[ˈdiːteilz]	Einzelheiten
no (not)–either	[ˈaiðə*]	auch nicht
electrician	[ilekˈtriʃən]	Elektriker

Lesson 11B

simple		einfach
She can cope with any problem.	[kəup]	Sie kann mit jedem Problem fertig werden.
electricity	[ilekˈtrisiti]	Elektrizität
to be attached to	[əˈætʃt]	befestigt; festgemacht an
terminal block	[ˈtəːminəl ˈblɔk]	Lüsterklemme
clamp	[klæmp]	Klemme; Halterung; Kabelschelle
tiny	[ˈtain|i]	winzig
to strip off		abstreifen
sheathing	[ˈʃiːðiŋ]	Umhüllung; Schutzsicht
strand	[strænd]	Faser
to touch	[tʌtʃ]	sich berühren; berühren
tool kit	[kit]	Werkzeugtasche; -kasten
minor	[ˈmainə*]	klein; unbedeutend
insulated handles	[ˈinsjuleitid]	isolierte Griffe
insulation	[ˌinsjuˈleiʃən]	Isolierung
as well as *R*		außerdem auch
insulator	[ˈinsjuleitə*]	Isolator
to insulate	[ˈinsjuleit]	isolieren
insulating tape	[teip]	Isolierband
to isolate/isolation	[ˈaisəuleit; ˌaisəuˈleiʃən]	isolieren = trennen von; absondern
torch	[tɔːtʃ]	Taschenlampe
to prefer	[priˈfə*]	vorziehen
preferably	[ˈprefərəb|li]	vorzugsweise; am besten; - liebsten
wire stripper (insulation stripping pliers)	[ˈwaiə ˈstripə*]	Abisolierzange
to remove	[riˈmuːv]	abziehen; entfernen
to damage	[ˈdæmidʒ]	beschädigen

Lesson 12A

domestic electricity	[dəuˈmestik]	Haushaltsstrom
electric current, power	[ˈkʌrənt] [ˈpauə*]	elektrischer Strom
a.c. (alternating current)	[ˈɔːltəneitiŋ]	Wechselstrom
voltage/volt	[ˈvəultidʒ/vɔlt]	el. Spannung; Volt
d.c. (direct current)	[diˈrekt]	Gleichstrom
three-phase current	[feiz]	Drehstrom
power current		Starkstrom
weak current; low voltage c.		Schwachstrom
to complete	[kəmˈpliːt]	schließen; vervollständigen
to break, broke, broken		unterbrechen; zerbrechen
electric heater	[hiːtə*]	el. Heizgerät
apart from		abgesehen von
consumption of current	[kənˈsʌmpʃən]	Stromverbrauch
to be annoying	[əˈnɔiiŋ]	ärgerlich sein
short circuit	[ˈsəːkit]	Kurzschluß
to blow (fuse)		rausspringen (einer Sicherung)
weak	[wiːk]	schwach
fuse box		Sicherungskasten
plug	[plʌg]	Stecker; Stöpsel
to rewire	[ˈriːwaiə*]	Sicherungsdraht erneuern
ampere	[ˈæmpɛə*]	Ampere
fixed appliance	[fikst əˈplaiəns]	fest montiertes Gerät

Lesson 12B

to flow		fließen
cable	[ˈkeib|l]	Kabel
live wire	[laiv ˈwaiə*]	stromführendes Kabel
neutral wire	[ˈnjuːtrəl ˈwaiə*]	Nulleiter
source of power	[sɔːs; ˈpauə*]	Stromquelle
to pass		durchgehen
earth wire	[ˈəːθ ˈwaiə*]	Erdleitung; Erdung; Masse
to connect	[kəˈnekt]	verbinden; anschließen
connection		Anschluß (el.)
exposed	[iksˈpəuzd]	äußerlich sichtbar
metalwork	[ˈmetlwəːk]	Metallfassung; -Rahmen
shrouded contact plug	[ˈʃraudid ˈkɔntækt plʌg]	Schutzkontakt; -(Schuko) -Stecker

Lesson 13A

light switch		Lichtschalter
to expect	[iks'pekt]	annehmen; erwarten
rocker switch	['rɔkə*]	Kippschalter
to mean		meinen; beabsichtigen
pull-cord switch		Zugschalter (Kordelzug-)
shockproof	['ʃɔkpru:f]	schlag (el.) –; stoßgesichert
extension lead	[iks'tenʃən li:d]	Verlängerungsschnur; -Leitung
extension flex (cord)	[fleks]	Verlängerungskabel (gebrauchsfertig)
cable socket	['keibl ˌsɔkit]	Kabel (Leitungs-)fassung
lamp plug	['læmp plʌg]	Lampenstecker
socket outlet	['autlet]	elektr. Anschlußstelle
socket panel	['pæn|l]	Tischsteckdose (mehrf. Anschluß)
additional	[ə'di|ʃənl]	zusätzlich
power outlet		Stromanschlußstelle
brochure	['brəuʃjuə*]	Broschüre
complete	[kəm'pli:t]	vollständig
fittings	['fitiŋz]	Armaturen; Beschläge
accessories	[ək'sesəriz]	Zubehör
to mend		flicken; reparieren
to wire a plug	[plʌg]	einen Stecker an ein Kabel anschließen
to plug		hineinstecken (Stecker; Stöpsel)
rule	[ru:l]	hier: Regel
A good pocket-knife always comes in handy. *R*		Ein gutes Taschenmesser kommt immer gelegen.
urgent	['ə:dʒənt]	dringend

Lesson 13B

to unscrew		losschrauben; aufschrauben
cord grip	['kɔ:d grip]	Kabelklemme – (Klammer)
terminal	['tə:minəl]	Anschlußklemme; Verbindungsklemme
to wind, wound –	[waind, waund –]	wickeln

covering (sheathing)	[ˈkʌvəriŋ] [ˈʃi:ðiŋ]	Überzug; Umhüllung
bare wire	[bɛə waiə*]	blanker Draht
flex (flexible cord)	[ˈfleksibl kɔ:d]	Anschlußkabel für el. Geräte
stray	[strei]	lose; nicht verbunden
plug over	[ˈkʌvə*]	Deckel des Steckers

Lesson 14A

to be definite	[ˈdefinit]	entschieden (eine Sache ist e.)
atomic power station	[əˈtɔmik ˈpauə ˈsteiʃən]	Atomkraftwerk
bank		Ufer
fellows	[ˈfeləuz]	Arbeitskollegen; Jungens
He has a safe car, but it uses a lot of petrol. That's the other side of the coin. *R*		Er hat ein sicheres Auto, aber es verbraucht viel Benzin. Das ist die Kehrseite der Medaille.
ugly	[ˈʌgl|i]	häßlich
to spoil	[spɔil]	verderben
landscape	[ˈlænskeip]	Landschaft
cooling tower	[ˈku:liŋ ˈtauə*]	Kühlturm
chimney	[ˈtʃimni]	Schornstein
district	[ˈdistrikt]	Gebiet; Bezirk
government	[ˈgʌvənmənt]	Regierung
He always sticks to his principles. *R*		Er bleibt seinen Grundsätzen immer treu.
energy	[ˈenədʒ|i]	Energie
sufficient	[səˈfiʃənt]	genügend
uranium	[juˈreinjəm]	Uran
nuclear fission	[ˈnju:kliə* ˈfiʃən]	Kernspaltung
sketch	[sketʃ]	Skizze
below	[biˈləu]	unter; unterhalb
It just doesn't make any sense to me. *R*	[sens]	Daraus werde ich nicht schlau.
His boss fired him. He had no other choice. *R*	[tʃɔis]	Sein Chef feuerte ihn. Ihm blieb keine andere Wahl.
Of course he has to pay the fine. After all, the accident was his fault. *R*		Natürlich muß er die Strafe bezahlen. Schließlich war der Unfall seine Schuld.

reactor	[ri(:)ˈæktə*]	Reaktor (Atom)
fuel rods		Brennstäbe
to contain	[kənˈtein]	enthalten
pellets	[ˈpelits]	Kügelchen
reaction/to react	[ri(:)ˈækʃən; ri(:)ˈækt]	Reaktion; reagiern
to heat up		aufheizen
to produce	[prəˈdju:s]	produzieren
production	[prəˈdʌkʃən]	Produktion
steam	[sti:m]	Dampf
to explode	[iksˈpləud]	explodieren
physicist	[ˈfizisist]	Physiker
chain reaction	[tʃein-riˈækʃən]	Kettenreaktion
to retard	[riˈtɑ:d]	verzögern; abbremsen
as it were *R*		sozusagen
radioactivity	[ˈreidiəuækˈtiviti]	Radioaktivität
radiation/to radiate	[ˌreidiˈeiʃən; ˈreidieit]	Strahlung; strahlen
x-rays	[ˈeksˈreiz]	Röntgenstrahlen
on the whole *R*		im großen und ganzen
atomic pile	[pail]	Atommeiler
gigantic	[dʒaiˈgæntik]	riesig; gigantisch
concrete	[ˈkəŋkri:t]	Beton
inevitable	[inˈevitəbl]	unvermeidlich
to rise, rose, risen		ansteigen (Temperatur)
progress	[ˈprəugres]	Fortschritt

Lesson 14B

generator	[ˈdʒenəreitə*]	Generator
mountainous	[ˈmauntinəs]	bergig
water turbine	[ˈtə:bin]	Wasserturbine
hydro-electric power station	[ˈhaidrəu-]	Wasserkraftwerk
furnace	[ˈfə:nis]	Ofen (Industrie-Zentralheizung)
beneath	[biˈni:θ]	unter; darunter
steam turbine	[ˈtə:bin]	Dampfturbine
to pass through		durchlaufen; durchgehen
transformer	[trænsˈfɔ:mə*]	Transformator
to transform	[trænsˈfɔ:m]	umspannen
to change up		hier: hochspannen (Strom)
power line		Hochspannungsleitung
pylon	[ˈpailən]	Hochspannungsmast

sub-station	[ˈsʌbˈsteiʃ|ən]	hier: Umspannwerk
to step down		Stromspannung verringen
industrial society	[inˈdʌstriəl] səˈsaiəti]	Industriegesellschaft
pollution	[pəˈluːʃən]	Verschmutzung
to pollute	[pəˈluːt]	verschmutzen
to release	[riˈliːs]	hier: einlassen; abfließen lassen

Lesson 15 A

cassette recorder	[kəˈset riˈkɔːdə*]	Kassettenrecorder
(tape) recorder		Tonbandgerät
to record	[riˈkɔːd]	aufzeichnen, aufnehmen
The police were at the scene of the accident in no time. *R*		Die Polizei war im Nu am Unfallort.
It takes a little longer to repair a foreign car. *R*		Es dauert ein bißchen länger, ein ausländisches Auto zu reparieren.
record player	[ˈrekɔːd.pleiə*]	Plattenspieler
speaker	[ˈspiːkə*]	Lautsprecher
stylus	[ˈstailəs]	Stift; Nadel (Plattenspieler)
waltz	[wɔːls]	Walzer
tape	[teip]	Tonband
lid		Deckel
properly	[ˈprɔpə*li]	ordentlich
spring		Feder
firm, firmly	[fəːm]	fest
it might do *R*		es könnte gehen
to stay closed	[klouzd]	zu bleiben; geschlossen bleiben
to leave s.th.		hier: etwas bleiben lassen
to fumble	[ˈfʌmb/l]	fummeln
to imagine s.th.	[iˈmædʒin]	sich etwas vorstellen
to appreciate	[əˈpriːʃieit]	schätzen

Lesson 15B

What's on at the cinema tonight? *R*		Was läuft heute abend im Kino?

to believe	[bi'li:v]	annehmen; vermuten
although	[ɔ:l'ðəu]	obwohl
to flicker	['flikə*]	flimmern
a few times		ein paarmal
sound	[saund]	Ton; Klang
tube (picture tube)	[tju:b]	Bildröhre
transistor	[træn'sistə*]	Transistor
channel	['tʃæn|l]	Kanal (TV)
channel selector	[si'lektə*]	Kanalwählschalter
to tune (tuning)	[tju:n]	abstimmen; Abstimmung (Sender)
slightly	['slaitli]	leicht; etwas; ein bißchen
to improve	[im'pru:v]	sich bessern; verbessern
brightness	['braitnis]	Helligkeit
contrast	['kɔntrɑ:st]	Kontrast
set		Gerät (TV; Radio)
controls	[kən'trəulz]	hier: Bedienungstasten; -Knöpfe
screen	[skri:n]	Bildschirm

Alphabetisches Register des Wortschatzes

Englisch–Deutsch

A

absolutely	ˈæbsəluːtli	völlig	6B
to accelerate	əkˈseləreit	beschleunigen	5B
accelerator pedal	əkˈseləreitə* pedl	Gaspedal	5B
access point	ˈækses	Autobahnauffahrt	9B
accessories	əkˈsesəriz	Zubehör	13A
accident	ˈæksidənt	Unfall, Zufall	8B
additional	əˈdiʃənl	zusätzlich	13A
to adjust	əˈdʒʌst	einstellen, regulieren	2B
adjusting knob	əˈdʒʌstiŋ nɔb	Stellknopf, Regulierknopf	5B
advert	ˈædvərt	Zeitungs-, Illustr.-Anzeige (Kurzform)	1B
advertisement	ədˈvəːtismənt	Zeitungs-, Illustr.-Anzeige	
advice	ədˈvais	Ratschlag	2A
aerial	ˈɛəriəl	Antenne	5A
after all *R*		schließlich; letzen Endes *R*	14A
to agree (with)	əˈgriː	zustimmen	11A
alternating current	ˈɔltəneitiŋ ˈkʌrənt	Wechselstrom	12A
although	ˈɔːlˈðəu	obwohl	15B
ampere	ˈæmpɛə*	Ampere	12A
to be annoying	əˈnɔiiŋ	ärgerlich sein (etwas ist ä.)	12A
anyway *R*		jedenfalls, sowieso, wie dem auch sei *R*	3A
apart (to keep a.)	əˈpɑːt	auseinander halten	9B
apart from		abgesehen von	12A
appliance	əˈplaiəns	Gerät (el.)	11A
to appreciate	əˈpriːʃieit	schätzen	15A
apprentice	əˈprentis	Lehrling	4B
to approach	əˈprəutʃ	sich nähern	8B
architect	ˈɑːkitekt	Architekt	11A
arm rest		Armstütze, Armlehne	5B
as it were *R*		sozusagen *R*	14A
as well as *R*		sowie auch, und außerdem noch *R*	8A 11B

ashtray	ˈæʃtrei	Aschenbecher	5B
asleep (to fall a.)		einschlafen	9B
to assemble	əˈsembl	zusammensetzen	3C
assembly line	əˈsembli lain	Fließband	10B
atomic	əˈtɔmik	atom-, atomar	14A
atomic pile	pail	Atommeiler	14A
atomic power station	ˈpauə ˈsteiʃən	Atomkraftwerk	14A
to be attached	əˈtætʃt	befestigt sein	11B
attendant	əˈtendənt	Wärter, Diensthabender	8A
automatic	ˌɔːtəˈmætik	automatisch	3B
automatic transmission	trænzˈmiʃən	Getriebeautomatik	5B

B

bank		Ufer	14A
bare wire	ˌbɛə ˈwaiə	blanker Draht	13B
bargain	ˈbɑːgin	günstiges Angebot; Sonderangebot	1B
basic (equipment)	ˈbeisik iˈkwipmənt	grundlegend (Grundausrüstung)	2A
beam (dipped b.)	biːm, dipt	Abblendlicht	5A
beam (full b.)		Fernlicht	5A
beginner	biˈginə*	Anfänger	3B
to believe	biˈliːv	annehmen; glauben	15B
below	biˈləu	unter; unterhalb	14A
beneath	biˈniːθ	unter; darunter	14B
bench (work bench)	bentʃ	Werkbank	2A
bend		Kurve	8B
better (you had better) *R*		du solltest lieber *R*	10B
bill		Rechnung	2A
bit	bit	Bohrer (Einsatz)	1A
to blow (fuse)		rausspringen (Sicherung)	12A
blimey *R*	ˈblaimi	Menschenskind! *R*	6B
board	bɔːd	Brett; Tafel	1A
body		Karosserie	5A
boiler	bɔilə*	Heizkessel	4B
bolt	bəult	Bolzen; Schraube	2B
bonnet	ˈbɔnit	Motorhaube	5A
bookcase	ˈbukkeis	Bücherschrank	1A
boot	buːt	Kofferraum	5A
to bore	bɔː*	maschinell bohren	3B
boring tool	ˈbɔːriŋ tuːl	Bohrmeißel	3B
bottom gear	ˈbɔtəm giə	erster Gang	6A
brake	breik	Bremse	5A

to brake		bremsen	5B
brake lights		Bremslichter	5A
brake pedal	ˈpedl	Bremspedal	5B
brand-new	brænd	nagelneu	8B
to break	breik	kaputt gehen	3C
to break		unterbrechen (el.)	12A
breakdown		Panne	9A
to be broken	ˈbrəukən	kaputt sein	3C
brightness	ˈbraitnis	Helligkeit	15B
brochure	ˈbrəuʃjuə*	Broschüre	13A
brow (hill)	brau	Hügelkuppe	8B
bulb	bʌlb	Glühbirne	6B
bumper	ˈbʌmpə*	Stoßstange	5A
button	ˈbʌtən	Knopf	3B
by the way *R*		übrigens *R*	2B

C

cable	keibl	Kabel; Leitung	12B
cable socket	keibl ˈsɔkit	Kabelsteckdose; Kupplung	13A
canteen	kænˈtiːn	Kantine	4B
cap (petrol c., valve c.)	kæp	Kappe; Verschluß	5A
cap nut	nʌt	Hutmutter	2B
car	kɑː	Auto	3A
car park		Parkplatz	9B
carburettor	ˈkɑːbjuretə*	Vergaser	8A
caretaker	ˈkɛə.teikə*	Hausmeister	4A
carriageway	ˈkæridʒwei	Fahrbahn (Autobahnseite)	9B
case (in case)	ˈkeis	falls	9A
cassette recorder	kəˈset riˈkɔːdə*	Kassettenrekorder	15A
cause	kɔːz	Ursache	9B
cautiously	ˈkɔːʃəsli	vorsichtig	8B
ceiling	ˈsiːliŋ	Zimmerdecke	11A
central heating	ˈsentrəl ˈhiːtiŋ	Zentralheizung	4A
centre (center) d.i.y.	ˈsentə	Heimwerkermarkt	1A
chain reaction	tʃein riˈækʃən	Kettenreaktion	14A
to change	tʃeindʒ	(aus-)wechseln	7B
to change (up, down)		schalten (Auto)	6A
to change up		hochspannen (el. Strom)	14B
channel	ˈtʃænl	Kanal (TV)	15B
channel selector	siˈlektə*	Kanalwählschalter	15B
chap	tʃæp	Bursche	4B

to charge	tʃɑːdʒ	laden (Batterie)	8A
chassis	ˈʃæsi	Fahrgestell	5A
to check	tʃek	durchgehen; überprüfen	2B
to check		durchsprechen; beraten	11A
chemical	ˈkemikəl	Chemie = chemisch	4B
chimney	ˈtʃimni	Schornstein	14A
chisel	ˈtʃizl	Meißel	1A
to chisel		meißeln	1A
choice	ˈtʃɔis	Wahl (Auswahl)	14A
to choose	tʃuːz	aussuchen; auswählen	1A
circuit	ˈsəːkit	Stromkreis	11A
clamp	klæmp	Klemme; Halterung	11B
clerk	klɑːk	Büroangestellter	2B
clockwise	ˈklɔkwaiz	im Uhrzeigersinn	6A
close	kləus	dicht; nahe	9B
to close	kləuz	schließen	10A
clutch pedal	klʌtʃ ˈpedl	Kupplungspedal	5B
coal mine	ˈkəul main	Kohlenbergwerk	4B
coat	kəut	Anstrich	1B
coat (top coat)		Deckanstrich; Lackierung	1B
coil	kɔil	Zündspule	10A
combustion chamber	kəmˈbʌstʃən ˈtʃeimbə*	Brennkammer; Verbrennungsraum	10A 14A
combustion engine	ˈendʒin	Verbrennungsmotor	10A
to come off		abgehen (Mutter; Rad etc.)	2B
common sense	ˈkɔmən sens	gesunder Menschenverstand	8B
to complete	kəmˈpliːt	schließen (Stromkreis)	12A
complete		vollständig	13A
complicated	ˈkɔmplikeitid	kompliziert	3C
to compress	kəmˈpres	zusammendrücken	10A
compression	kəmˈpreʃən	Verdichtung	10A
concrete	ˈkɔŋkriːt	Beton	14A
confusing	kənfˈjuːziŋ	verwirrend	9A
to congratulate	kənˈgrætjuleit	gratulieren	8B
congratulation	kənˌgrætjuˈleiʃən	Glückwunsch	8B
to connect	kəˈnekt	verbinden; anschließen (el.)	12B
connecting rod	rɔd	Pleuelstange	10A
connection	kəˈnekʃən	Anschluß (el.)	12B
constant	ˈkɔnstənt	gleichbleibend	4B
to consume	kənˈsjuːm	verbrauchen	7A
consumption	kənˈsʌmpʃən	Verbrauch	7A

consumption of current	ˈkʌrənt	Stromverbrauch	12A
contact breaker points	ˈkɔntækt·breikə*	Unterbrecherkontakte	8A
to contain	kənˈtein	enthalten	14A
contrast	ˈkɔntrɑ:st	Kontrast (TV)	15B
control system	kənˈtrəul ˈsistim	Steuerungsanlage	4B
controls	kənˈtrəulz	Bedienungstasten, -knöpfe	15B
cooker	ˈkukə*	Elektroherd	11A
cooling tower	ˈku:liŋ ˈtauə	Kühlturm	14A
to cope with	kəup	zurechtkommen mit; fertigwerden mit	11B
cord grip	kɔ:d grip	Kabelklemme	13B
corporation	kɔ:pəˈreiʃen	Gesellschaft; Körperschaft	4B
cover	ˈkʌvə*	Deckel	13B
covering	ˈkʌvəriŋ	Überzug; Isolierschicht	13B
crankshaft	ˈkræŋkʃɑ:ft	Kurbelwelle	10A
crossing		Übergang	8B
crosswise	ˈkrɔswaiz	über Kreuz	7B
current (electric c.)	ˈkʌrənt	el. Strom	12A
customer	ˈkʌstəmə*	Kunde	7A
to cut down		einschränken; sparen an	2A
cylindrical	siˈlindrikəl	zylindrisch	3B

D

to damage	ˈdæmidʒ	beschädigen	11B
dangerous	ˈdeindʒrəs	gefährlich	6B
dashboard	ˈdæʃbɔ:d	Armaturenbrett	5B
dealer (car d.)	ˈdi:lə*	Händler (Autohändler)	7A
deepfreezer	ˈdi:pˈfri:zə*	Tiefkühltruhe	11A
definite	ˈdefinit	entschieden	14A
to demand	diˈmɑ:nd	(an-)fordern	10B
dent		Beule	5A
to depress	diˈpres	treten; durchtreten (Kupplung; Gas)	6A
details	ˈdi:teilz	Einzelheiten	11A
to develop	diˈvələp	entwickeln	4B
different	ˈdifrənt	unterschiedlich	1A
difficult	ˈdifikəlt	schwierig	8B
dipswitch	ˈdipswitʃ	Abblendlichtschalter	5B
direct current	diˈrekt ˈkʌrənt	Gleichstrom	12A
direction	diˈrekʃən	Richtung	9B

directions for use	di'rekʃənz	Gebrauchsanweisung	3C
to disassemble	'disəsembl	auseinandernehmen	3C
to discharge	'distʃɑ:dʒ	entladen (Batterie)	8A
dishwasher	'diʃwɔʃə*	Geschirrspülautomat	11A
district	'distrikt	Gebiet; Bezirk	14A
distribution box	ˌdistri'bju:ʃən	Verteilerdose	11A
distributor head	dis'tribjutə*	Verteilerkopf	10A
domestic electricity	dəu'mestik ilek'trisiti	Haushaltsstrom	12A
door handle	'hændl	Türgriff	5A
to draw		ziehen; ansaugen	10A
dreadful	dredful	schrecklich	9B
to drill		bohren	1A
drill		Bohrer (el.)	1A
to drive		fahren (Auto)	5B
driver's seat	'draivəz si:t	Fahrersitz	5B
driving licence	'laisəns	Führerschein	8B
driving test		Fahrprüfung	8B
dull	dʌl	langweilig	10B

E

earth wire	'ə:θ 'waiə	Erdleitung	12B
egg boiler	'bɔilə*	Eierkocher	11A
either (not e.; no … e.)	'aiðə*	auch nicht	11A
elderly	'eldəli	älter, ältlich	8B
electric	i'lektrik	elektrisch	1A, 11A
electrician	ilək'triʃən	Elektriker; E.-Installateur	11A
electricity	ilək'trisiti	Elektrizität	11B
end (in the e.) *R*		letzten Endes; schließlich *R*	4A
energy	'enədʒi	Energie	14A
engine	'endʒin	Motor	3A
engineer	ˌendʒi'niə*	Ingenieur	4B
enough	i'nʌf	genügend	6B
enthusiast (d.i.y.)	in'θju:ziæst	Heimwerker; Bastler	1A
equipment	i'kwipmənt	Ausrüstung; Geräte	2A
estate car	i'steitkɑ:*	Kombiwagen	4A
ever		jemals	8B
exactly	ig'zæktli	genau(-so)	6B
to exceed	ik'si:d	überschreiten (Geschwindigkeit)	9A

except for	ik'sept	außer	9A
excited	ik'saitid	aufgeregt	4B
exhaust	ig'zɔ:st	Auspuff; Ausstoß (Gas)	10A
exhaust pipe		Auspuffrohr	5A
exhaust stroke	strəuk	Ausstoßtakt (Motor)	10A
exit	'eksit	Ausfahrt; Ausgang (Autobahn)	9B
to expect	iks'pekt	annehmen; erwarten	13A
expensive	iks'pensiv	teuer	9A
experience	iks'piəriəns	Erfahrung	3B
experienced	iks'piəriənst	erfahren	3B
expert	'ekspə:t	Fachmann	2A
to explain	iks'plein	erklären	4B
to explode	iks'pləud	explodieren	14A
explosion	iks'pləuʒən	Explosion	10A
explosive	iks'pləusiv	explosiv	10A
exposed	iks'pəuzd	äußerlich sichtbar	12B
extension flex	iks'tenʃən fleks	Verlängerungskabel	13A
extension lead	iks'tenʃən li:d	Verlängerungsschnur-Leitung	13A
exterior	eks'tiəriə*	äußerlich; das Äußere	5A
extras	'ekstrəz	Extras (Auto)	7A
eye (to keep an e. on) s.th. – s.b. *R*		etwas, -jemandem im Auge behalten *R*	3C

F

to face		plandrehen (stirndrehen)	3B
factory	'fæktəri	Fabrik	3A
fan		Gebläse; Ventilator	5B
to fasten	'fɑ:sn	einhaken; befestigen	6A
fault	fɔ:lt	Defekt; Fehler	4A
fellows	'feləuz	Arbeitskollegen	14A
fender (U.S.)	'fendə*	Kotflügel	5A
file	fail	Feile; Akte	2A
to file		feilen; Akten ablegen	2A
filling station (U.S.)	'filiŋ 'steiʃən	Tankstelle	3A
fine		Geldstrafe	6B
finished	'finiʃt	fertig; erledigt	8A
firm(-ly)	fə:m	fest	15A
the first time *R*		das erstemal *R*	7B
to fit		passen; montieren	2B
fitter	'fitə*	Monteur	3C
fittings	'fitiŋz	Armaturen; Beschläge	13A

to fix		einsetzen; anbringen; befestigen	3B
to fix		in Ordnung bringen; reparieren	6B
fixed appliance	əˈplaiəns	fest montiertes el. Gerät	12A
flat		leer (Batterie)	8A
flat		platt (Reifen)	8A
flex (flexible cord)	ˈfleksibl kɔːd	Anschlußkabel	13B
to flicker	ˈflikə*	flimmern	15B
to flow		fließen	12B
fluorescent light	fluəˈresnt	Leuchtröhre; Neonlicht	11A
foglight		Nebelleuchte	5A
foreman	ˈfɔːmən	Werkmeister; Vorarbeiter	4B
to form-turn		formdrehen	3B
frame-saw	ˈfreim|sɔː	Bügelsäge	2B
fretsaw	ˈfret|sɔː	Laubsäge	2B
frequent	ˈfriːkwənt	häufig	9B
fridge (refrigerator)	ˈfridʒ	Kühlschrank	11A
fuel	ˈfjuəl	Kraftstoff; Treibstoff	7A
fuel gauge	geidʒ	Kraftstoffanzeiger (Benzinuhr)	5A
fuel rods	rɔd	Brennstäbe (Atomkraftwerk)	14A
to fumble	ˈfʌmbl	fummeln	15A
function	ˈfʌnkʃən	Funktion	3B
funny	ˈfʌni	komisch; spaßig	3A
furnace	ˈfəːnis	Ofen (Industrie; Zentralheizung)	14B
fuse	fjuːz	Sicherung (el.)	6B
fuse box		Sicherungskasten	12A

G

gallon	ˈgælən	Gallone (4,54 Liter)	7A
garage	ˈgærɑːʒ	Reparaturwerkstatt; Garage	3A
to gather speed	ˈgæðə* spiːd	Fahrt aufnehmen; schneller fahren	6A
gauge (gage U.S.)	geidʒ	Meßgerät	4B
gear	ˈgiə*	Getriebe	10A
gear lever	ˈliːvə*	Schalthebel (Auto)	5B

generator	ˈdʒenəreitə*	Generator	14B
generator warning light	ˈwɔːniŋ	Lichtmaschinenanzeiger	5B
gently	ˈdʒentli	sachte; sanft	6A
to get on		zurechtkommen; vorankommen	8A
geyser (hot water g.)	ˈgaizə*	Heißwassergerät	4A
gigantic	dʒaiˈgæntik	gigantisch; riesig	14A
gimlet	ˈgimlit	Nagelbohrer	2B
at a glance *R*	glɑːns	auf einen Blick *R*	4B
at first glance *R*		auf den ersten Blick *R*	4B
to glare	ˈglɛə*	strahlen; hell leuchten	4A
glove compartment	glʌv kəmˈpɑːtmənt	Handschuhfach	5B
government	ˈgʌvənmənt	Regierung	14A
grease	griːs	Schmierfett	3C
to grease		abschmieren (Fett)	3C
groove	gruːv	Nut; Rinne	3B
guarantee	ˌgærənˈtiː	Garantie	7A
to guide	gaid	einweisen (ein Fahrzeug in den Verkehr)	6A

H

hacksaw	ˈhæksɔː	Eisensäge	2B
hammer	ˈhæmə*	Hammer	1A
to hammer		hämmern; einschlagen	1A
hand (on the one h. – on the other h.) *R*		einerseits – andererseits *R*	2A
handbrake	breik	Handbremse	5B
handles	ˈhændlz	Griffe	11B
handsaw		Handsäge; Fuchsschwanz	2B
handshield	ˈhændʃiːld	Schweißschirm	4A
to be handy *R*	ˈhændy	griffbereit *R*	3C
to come in handy *R*		gelegen kommen *R*	13A
hardly ever *R*		kaum jemals *R*	11A
hardwareshop	ˈhɑːdwɛəʃɔp	Eisenwarenhandlung	2B
harp	hɑːp	Harfe	3A
hazard flasher	ˈhæzəd flæʃə*	Lichthupe	5B
head		Kopf (Schraube; Bolzen)	2B
headlights		Scheinwerfer (Auto)	5A
headrest		Kopfstütze	5B
to heat up		aufheizen	14A
heated	ˈhiːtid	beheizt	5A

heater	ˈhiːtə*	Heizgerät (el.)	12A
heater switch	switʃ	Heizungsschalter	5B
helicopter	ˈhelikəptə*	Hubschrauber	9A
helmet	ˈhelmit	Schutzhelm	4A
hexagonal	ˈheksægənl	sechseckig	2B
highway code	ˈhaiwei kəud	Straßenverkehrsordnung	8B
hilly	ˈhili	hügelig	9B
hinges	ˈhindʒiz	Scharniere	2B
hint	hint	Hinweis; Tip	2A, 8B
hoist	hɔist	Hebevorrichtung; Kran	10B
to hoist		hochziehen; hissen	10B
hole	həul	Loch	1B
hood (U.S.)	hud	Motorhaube	5A
horn	hɔːn	Hupe	5A
housekeeping money		Haushaltsgeld	2A
hub cap	hʌb	Radkappe	5A
hydro-electric power station	ˈhaidrəu iˈlektrik ˈpauə ˈsteiʃən	Wasserkraftwerk	14B

I

idea	aiˈdiə	Idee	3A
to ignite	igˈnait	zünden	10A
ignition key	igˈniʃən	Zündschlüssel	5B
ignition light = generator w. light		Lichtmaschinenanzeiger	5B
ignition switch		Zündschloß	5B
to imagine	iˈmædʒin	sich etwas vorstellen	15A
important	imˈpɔːtənt	wichtig	4B
to improve	imˈpruːv	sich bessern	15B
to indicate	ˈindikeit	anzeigen	4B
indicator	ˈindikeitə*	Anzeigegerät, Blinker (Auto)	4B, 5A
induction stroke	inˈdʌkʃən strəuk	Ansaugtakt	10A
industrial society	inˈdʌstriəl səˈsaiəti	Industriegesellschaft	14B
inevitable	inˈevitəbl	unvermeidlich	14A
to inflate	inˈfleit	aufpumpen	5A
inlet (valve)	ˈinlet vælv	Einlaß (Ventil)	10A
inside	ˈinˈsaid	drin; drinnen	8A
to install	inˈstɔːl	anbringen; installieren	4A
instinctively	inˈstiŋktivli	instinktiv	8B
instructions (set of i.)	inˈstrʌkʃənz	Montageanleitung (Bauanleitung)	1B

to insulate	ˈinsjuleit	isolieren (el.)	11B
insulating tape	teip	Isolierband	11B
insulation	ˌinsjuˈleiʃən	Isolierung	11B
insulator	ˈinsjuleitə*	Isolator	11B
interior	inˈtiəriə*	das Innere; innen	5B
interval	ˈintəvəl	Zeitabstand	3C
iron	ˈaiən	Eisen	2B
to isolate	ˈaisəuleit	isolieren; absondern	11B
isolation	ˌaisəuˈleiʃn	Isolation; Absonderung	11B
item (next item)	ˈaitəm	Punkt (Liste; Tagesordnung)	2B

J

jack (car jack)	dʒæk	Wagenheber	7B
to jack up		hochpumpen; heben (Auto)	7B
to join together	dʒɔin	miteinander verbinden; zusammenfügen	1B
joint		Verbindungsstelle, -stück; Fuge; Gelenk	1B
joint	dʒɔint	Muffe	4A
just	dʒʌst	bloß, eben, nur	3B, 9A

K

to keep apart	əˈpɑːt	auseinanderhalten; trennen	9B
to keep up with *R*		Schritt halten mit *R*	
kind (– of)		(eine) Art (von)	3B
knob	nɔb	Drehknopf	3B
kit (tool-; repair)		Tasche; Kasten	11B

L

lamp plug	ˈlæmp plʌg	Lampenstecker	13A
landscape	ˈlænskeip	Landschaft	14A
lane		Fahrspur (Autobahn)	9A
lathe	leið	Drehmaschine	3A
lawn mower	ˈlɔːn ˌməuə*	Rasenmäher	2B
lay-by		Haltestreifen, -platz (Autobahn)	9B
leaflet	ˈliːflit	Flugblatt	1B

leak	li:k	Leck; Riß	4A
at least	li:st	mindestens; wenigstens	11A
to leave s.th.		etwas bleiben lassen	15A
to leave s.th. to s.b.		etwas jemandem überlassen	3C
level	ˈlevl	Stand; Niveau	6A, 8A
lever	ˈli:və*	Hebel	3B
licence	ˈlaisəns	Zulassung	5A
lid		Deckel	5A, 15A
light switch		Lichtschalter	13A
live wire	ˌlaivˈwaiə*	stromführender Draht (Leitung)	12B
local	ˈləukəl	örtlich	2B
to lock	lɔk	zuschließen	4B
lock nut	nʌt	Kontermutter	2B
locksmith	ˈlɔksmiθ	Schlosser	4B
lorry	ˈlɔri	Lastwagen (Lkw)	9B
loose	ˈlu:s	lose; locker	2B
to loosen	ˈlu:sn	lösen (Mutter; Schraube)	2B
to lose, lost, lost	ˈlu:z; lɔst	verlieren	2B
lubricant	ˈlubrikənt	Schmieröl	3C
to lubricate	ˈlu:brikeit	abschmieren (Öl)	3C
to be lucky *R*		Glück haben *R*	7B

M

machine	məˈʃi:n	Maschine	3A
machinist	məˈʃi:nist	Maschinist	3B
main line	mein lain	Hauptfließband	10B
mains	meinz	Hauptleitung (Strom; Wasser; Gas)	4A
maintenance	ˈmeintənəns	Wartung (Auto; Maschine)	7A
manual choke	ˈmænjuəl tʃəuk	Starterklappe	5B
mark	mɑ:k	Markierung	1B
to mark		markieren	1B
material	məˈtiəriəl	Material	1A
(as a) matter of fact *R*		eigentlich *R*	3A
(a) matter of time *R*		eine Frage der Zeit *R*	8B
to mean		meinen; beabsichtigen	13A
measurements	ˈməʒəmənts	Maße	1B
mechanic	miˈkænik	Mechaniker	2A

to mend		flicken; reparieren	13A
metal	ˈmetl	Metall	3B
metalwork	ˈmetlwəːk	Metallfassung; Rahmen	12B
might (it might do) *R*		es könnte gehen *R*	15A
to mill		fräsen	3B
milling cutter	ˈmiliŋ ˈkʌtə*	Fräser (Teil der Fräsmaschine)	3B
milling machine	məˈʃiːn	Fräse	3B
minor	ˈmainə*	klein; unbedeutend	11B
motor-car	ˈməutəkɑː*	Auto	5A
motorist	ˈməutərist	Autofahrer; Kraftfahrer	8A
motorway	ˈməutəwei	Autobahn	9A
mountainous	ˈmauntinəs	bergig	14B
to move off		losfahren	6A
mudguard	ˈmʌdgɑːd	Kotflügel	5A

N

nail	neil	Nagel	1A
narrow	ˈnærəu	schmal; eng	9A
to need		benötigen; brauchen	1A
needle	niːdl	Nadel	4B
neutral gear	ˈnjuːtrəl giə*	Leerlauf	6A
neutral wire	ˈwaiə*	Nulleiter	12B
next door		nebenan	3A
nothing but		nichts als (-außer)	6B
not at all *R*		überhaupt nicht *R*	8A
nuclear fission	ˈnjuːkliə* ˈfiʃən	Kernspaltung	14A
number plate		Nummerschild	5A
nut	nʌt	Mutter	2B
to be nuts *R*	nuts	verrückt sein *R*	2B

O

odometer	əuˈdɔmitə*	Kilometerzähler	5B
official	əˈfiʃəl	amtlich	9A
office	ˈɔfis	Büro	2A
oil	ɔil	Öl	4B
oil level	ɔil levl	Ölstand	6A
to operate	ˈɔpəreit	bedienen (Maschine)	3A
operating instruction	ˈɔpəreitiŋ inˈstrʌkʃən	Bedienungsanleitung	3C

operation	ˌɔpəˈreiʃən	Arbeitsvorgang	3B
operator	ˈɔpəreitə*	Bediener (Maschine); tel. Vermittlung	3A
the other day *R*		neulich *R*	4A
outlet (valve)	autlet vælv	Auslaß (Ventil); Austritt (el.)	10A
to overload	ˈəuvəˈləud	überlasten; überladen (el.)	11A
to overtake		überholen (Verkehr)	6A
oxy-acetylene-cylinder	ˈɔksiəˈsetiliːn ˈsilində*	Sauerstoff-Azetylen-Flasche	4A

P

pace	peis	Tempo, Bewegung, Schritt	10B
to paint	peint	malen, streichen, lackieren	1B
to paper		tapezieren	1A
parking area (lot)	ˈɛəriə	Parkplatz	9B
parking light		Standlicht	5A
to pass		bestehen (Prüfung)	8B
to pass through		vorbeifahren, -gehen;	12B
		durchlaufen, -gehen (el.)	14B
passenger seat	ˈpæsindʒə*	Beifahrersitz	5B
patrol car	pəˈtrəul	Streifenwagen	9A
pedestrian	piˈdestrĭən	Fußgänger	8B
pellets	ˈpelits	Kügelchen	14A
personnel manager	ˌpəːsəˈnel ˈmænidʒə*	Personalchef	10B
perseverance	ˌpəːsiˈviərəns	Ausdauer	10B
petrol, (gas U.S.)	ˈpetrəl; gæs	Benzin	9B
petrol cap		Tankklappe, -verschluß	5A
three phase current	feiz ˈkʌrənt	Drehstrom	12A
physicist	ˈfizisist	Physiker	14A
picture (to put s.b. in the p.) *R*		jem. ein Bild vermitteln, informieren *R*	4B
piece		Bauteil; Einzelteil; Stück	1B
piece of material	məˈtiərĭəl	Werkstück	3B
pincers (pair of p.)	ˈpinsəz	Kneifzange	2B
pipe		Rohr	4A
pipeline	ˈpaiplain	Rohrleitung	4B
pipe system	ˈsistim	Rohrleitungsanlage	4B
piston	ˈpistən	Kolben (Mot.)	10A

(plain)-milling cutter	ˈplein ˌmiliŋ kʌtə*	Walzenfräser (Maschinenteil)	3B
plane	plein	Hobel	2B
to plane		hobeln (langhobeln); planieren	2B, 3B
planer (planing machine)	ˈpleinə*	Langhobelmaschine	3B
plant (steel-; car-; chemical-)	plɑːnt	Werke; große Fabrikanlage	4B, 10B
pliers (pair of p.)	ˈplaiəz	Kombizange	2B
plumber	ˈplʌmə*	Installateur (Wasser; Gas; Sanitär)	2B
plug	plʌg	Stecker; Stöpsel; Dübel	12A
to plug		hineinstecken; einstöpseln	13A
to pollute	pəˈluːt	verschmutzen	14B
pollution	pəˈluːʃən	Verschmutzung	14B
possible	ˈpɔsibl	möglich	11A
power	ˈpauə*	el. Strom (Umgangssprache)	12A
power current	ˈkurənt	Starkstrom	12A
power line	lain	Hochspannungsleitung	14B
power outlet	ˈautlet	Stromanschlußstelle	13A
power station	ˈsteiʃən	Kraftwerk	14A
power wrench	rentʃ	Preßluftschraubenschlüssel	10B
practical	ˈpræktikəl	praktisch	8B
prefabricated	ˈpriːˈfæbrikeitid	vorgefertigt	1B
to prefer	priˈfəː*	vorziehen	11B
preferably	ˈprefərəbli	vorzugsweise	11B
to press; press	pres	drücken; Presse	3B
pressure	ˈpreʃə*	Druck	4B
to prime	praim	grundieren	1B
primer	ˈpraimə*	Grundierung	1B
to process	ˈprəuses	bearbeiten; verarbeiten (Material)	3B
to produce	prəˈdjuːs	produzieren	14A
production	prəˈdʌkʃən	Produktion	14A
profile	ˈprəufail	Profil	3B
progress	ˈprəugres	Fortschritt	14A
to promise	ˈprɔmis	versprechen	3A
properly	ˈprɔpəli	ordentlich	15A
prospects	ˈprɔspekts	Zukunftsaussichten	4B
to protect from	prəˈtekt	schützen vor	4A
protective clothing	prəˈtektiv	Schutzkleidung	4A

pull-cord switch	ˈpul-kɔːd switʃ	Zugschalter	13A
to punch	pʌntʃ	stanzen; lochen	3B
punching machine	ˈpʌntʃiŋ	Stanze	3B
puncture	ˈpʌŋktʃə*	Reifenpanne; Platten	7B
to push in		reindrücken (Knopf)	3B
to push up		hochschieben (Hebel)	3B
tp put in		einspannen (Werkstück)	3B
to put s.th. right *R*		etwas in Ordnung bringen *R*	4A
pylon	ˈpailən	Hochspannungsmast	14B

Q

quarter	ˈkwɔːtə*	Viertel	6B
quite	kwait	ganz	8A

R

to radiate	ˈreidieit	strahlen	14A
radiation	ˌreidiˈeiʃən	Strahlung	14A
radiator grill	ˈreidieitə* gril	Kühlergitter	5A
radio	ˈreidiəu	Radio	5B
radioactivity	ˈreidiəuækˈtiviti	Radioaktivität	14A
rawl plug	rɔːl plʌg	Mauerdübel	2B
to react	ri(ː)ˈækt	reagieren	8B, 14A
reaction	ri(ː)ˈækʃən	Reaktion	14A
reactor	ri(ː)ˈæktə*	Reaktor	14A
rear fog light	ˈriə	Nebelschlußleuchte	5A
rear light		Rückleuchte	5A
rear-view mirror	ˈriə vjuː ˈmirə*	Rückblickspiegel	5A, 5B
rear window	ˈriə*	Heckscheibe (Fenster)	5A
to reassemble	ˈriːəˈsembl	wieder zusammensetzen	3C
receipt	riˈsiːt	Quittung	8A
to recharge	ˈriːˈtʃɑːdʒ	wieder aufladen (Batterie)	8A
reckless	ˈreklis	leichtfertig; unbesonnen	8B
to recommend	ˌrekəˈmend	empfehlen	9A
recommendation	ˌrekəmenˈdeiʃən	Empfehlung	9A
reconditioned	ˈriːkənˈdiʃənd	generalüberholt (Auto)	7A
to record	riˈkɔːd	aufnehmen; aufzeichnen	15A
record player	ˈrekɔːd ˌpleiə*	Plattenspieler	15A

recorder (tape r.)	riˈkɔːdə*	Tonbandgerät	15A
region	ˈriːdʒən	Gegend	9B
regular	ˈregjulə*	regelmäßig	3C
to regulate	ˈregjuleit	regeln; regulieren	3B
to release	riˈliːs	kommen lassen (Kupplung); lösen	6A
to release		einlassen; abfließen lassen	14B
release		Entriegelungshebel	5B
reliable	riˈlaiəbl	zuverlässig	4B
to rely on	riˈlai	sich verlassen auf	4B
to remove	riˈmuːv	abziehen; entfernen	11B
to renovate	ˈrenəuveit	renovieren	11A
to repair	riˈpɛə*	reparieren	1A
repair job		Reparatur	1A
to replace	riˈpleis	ersetzen	3C
to report (to)	riˈpɔːt	melden (bei); sich melden bei	10B
responsible	risˈpɔnsəbl	verantwortlich	4B
result	riˈzʌlt	Ergebnis	1B
resurfacing	ˈriːˈsəːfisiŋ	Erneuerung der Fahrbahn	9A
to retard	riˈtɑːd	verzögern, abbremsen	14A
to reverse	riˈvəːs	zurücksetzen (Auto)	6A
reverse gear	giə	Rückwärtsgang	6A
reversing light		Rückfahrscheinwerfer	5A
revolution	ˌrəvəˈluːʃən	Umdrehung	3B
to rewire	ˈriːˈwaiə*	Sicherungsdraht erneuern	12A
to ride		fahren (Rad; Moped)	6B
rig (drilling r.)		Bohrplattform	4B
rim		Felge	5A
to rise		ansteigen (Temperatur)	14A
road junction	roud ˈdʒʌŋkʃən	Straßenkreuzung	8B
road works		Straßenbauarbeiten	9A
rocker switch	ˈrɔkə* switʃ	Kippschalter	13A
roof	ruːf	Dach	5A
to rotate	rəuˈteit	sich drehen	3B
round bar steel	raund-bɑː-stiːl	Rundstahl	3B
routine	ruːˈtiːn	Routine; Gewohnheit	4B
rule	ruːl	Gliedermaßstab (Zollstock); Regel	1A, 13A
to run out of		ausgehen (Benzin; Geld)	6B
to run smoothly	ˈsmuːðli	normal (rund) laufen (Motor)	6A

running order (perfect r.o.)	ˈpəːfikt-ˈɔːdə*	absolut fahrbereit (Auto)	7A
rush hour	ˈrʌʃ-auə*	Spitzenverkehrszeit	8B

S

safety goggles	ˈseifti ˈgɔglz	Schutzbrille	4A
to save		sparen; retten	2A
saw		Säge	1A
to saw		sägen	1A
scale	skeil	Skala	4B
screen (TV)	skriːn	Bildschirm	15B
screwdriver	ˈskruːˌdraivə*	Schraubenzieher (-dreher)	1A
seat belt	siːt belt	Anschnallgurt	5B
seat belt buckle	ˈbʌkl	Gurtverriegelung	5B
second-hand		Gebraucht-	7A
sense (to make s.) *R*		einleuchten; schlau (klug) werden aus *R*	14A
to service	ˈsəviːs	pflegen, warten (Auto; Maschine)	7A
service		Inspektion	7A
service station	ˈsteiʃən	Tankstelle	3A
set		Satz (Werkzeuge)	1A
set (TV; radio)		Gerät (TV; Radio)	15B
to set (up)		einrichten (Werkstatt; Büro); Maschine	2A, 3B
several	ˈsevrəl	verschiedene; mehrere	2B
to shape	ʃeip	stoßen; kurzhobeln; formen	3B
shaper (shaping machine)	ˈʃeipə*	Waagerechtstoßmaschine, Kurzhobler	3B
sheathing	ˈʃiːðiŋ	Umhüllung; Schutzschicht	11B
shed	ʃed	Schuppen	2A
shelf	ʃelf	Regal(-brett)	1A
shell-end-milling	ˈʃel-end ˈmiliŋ	stirnfräsen	3B
shift	ʃift	Schicht (Arbeit)	10B
shockproof	ˈʃɔkpruːf	Schlag(-stoß)-gesichert	13A
short circuit	ˈsəːkit	Kurzschluß	12A
shoulder (hard sh.)	ˈʃouldə*	betonierter Seitenstreifen; Standspur Autobahn	9A

shrouded contact plug	ˈʃraudid ˈkɔntækt plʌg	Schukostecker	12B
to signal	ˈsignl	anzeigen	6A
silencer	ˈsailənsə*	Auspufftopf	5A
simple		einfach	11B
size	saiz	Größe; Maß	1B
size (to cut to size)		auf Maß schneiden	1B
sketch	sketʃ	Skizze	14A
skilful	ˈskilful	geschickt	2A
to slab mill	slæb mil	walzfräsen	3B
slack	slæk	locker; schlaff	7A
slightly	ˈslaitli	leicht; etwas; ein bißchen	15B
to slow down		Geschwindigkeit verringern	6A
so		also; deshalb	9A
socket	ˈsɔkit	Fassung (Glühbirne)	11A
socket outlet	ˈautlet	el. Anschlußstelle	13A
socket panel	ˈpænl	Mehrfachsteckdose (Leiste, Tischsteckdose)	13A
soft	sɔft	weich	4A
to solder	ˈsɔːldə*	löten	4A
solderer	ˈsɔːldərə*	Löter	4A
soldering gear	giə	Lötgerät	4A
soldering iron	ˈaiən	Lötkolben	4A
to sound	saund	klingen	8B
sound		Ton; Klang	15B
source of power	sɔːs-ˈpauə*	Stromquelle	12B
spacer	ˈspeisə*	Unterlegscheibe	2B
spanner	ˈspænə*	Schraubenschlüssel	2B
spare parts	ˈspɛə* pɑːts	Ersatzteile	3C
spare wheel	wiːl	Reservereifen	7B
spark	spɑːk	Funken	4A
sparking plugs	ˈspɑːkiŋ plʌgz	Zündkerzen	8A
speaker	ˈspiːkə*	Lautsprecher	15A
special	ˈspeʃəl	extra; bsonders	3B, 11A
speed	spiːd	Geschwindigkeit	3B, 6A
speeding	ˈspiːdiŋ	Geschwindkigkeitsüberschreitung	6B
speed limit	ˈlimit	Geschwindigkeitsbebegrenzung	9A
speedometer	spiˈdɔmitə*	Tachometer	5B
spindle	ˈspindl	Spindel (Bohr- und Fräsmaschine)	3B

to spoil	spɔil	verderben	14A
spoilsport	ˈspɔilspɔːt	Spielverderber	2B
spot welding	ˈspɔt ˌweldiŋ	Punktschweißen	10B
spring		Feder	15A
square	skwεə*	viereckig; Viereck	2B
to stall	stɔːl	abwürgen (Motor)	8B
to start		anlassen, starten	3B
to start		anspringen (Motor)	6A
to start off		losfahren	8B
starter	ˈstɑːtə*	Anlasser	6A
station wagon (U.S)	ˈsteiʃən ˌwægən	Kombiwagen	4A
statistics	stəˈtistiks	statistische Angaben	8B
to stay (to stay the night)		bleiben; übernachten	9B
to stay closed	klouzd	zu bleiben; geschlossen bleiben	15A
steam	stiːm	Dampf	14A
steam turbine	ˈtəːbin; ˈtəːbain	Dampfturbine	14B
steel plate	ˈstiːl ˈpleit	Stahlplatte	4A
to step down		Spannung runterschalten (el.)	14B
steering		Lenkung	7A
steering wheel	ˈstiəriŋwiːl	Lenkrad	5B
to stick to *R*		bleiben bei (Grundsatz)	14A
stiff		steif	7A
to stop		abstellen; halten	3B
stop cock	kɔk	Absperrhahn	4A
stop nut	nʌt	Verschlußmutter	2B
straight	streit	gerade	1A
straight turning	ˈtuːniŋ	langdrehen	3B
strand	strænd	Faser	11B
stray	strei	lose (Faser; Draht)	13B
to strip off		abstreifen	11B
stroke	strəuk	Takt; Hub (Motor)	10A
stylus	ˈstailəs	Stift; Nadel (Plattenspieler)	15A
sub station	ˈsʌb ˈsteiʃən	Umspannwerk	14B
sufficient	səˈfiʃənt	genügend	14A
to suggest	səˈdʒest	vorschlagen	2A, 11A
suggestion	səˈdʒestʃən	Vorschlag	11A
supply (hot water s.)	səˈplai	Versorgungsanlage (Heiß-Wasser)	4A
to suppose	səˈpəuz	vermuten	6B
surface	ˈsəːfis	Fahrbahndecke; Oberfläche	9A

surprised	səˈpraizd	überrascht	2A
switch	switʃ	Schalter	3B

T

to take longer *R*		länger dauern; mehr Zeit brauchen *R*	15A
to take s.b. round		jem. herumführen	4B
tank	tæŋk	Kessel; Tank	4B
tap	tæp	Wasserhahn	4A
tape	teip	Tonband	15A
technical	ˈteknikəl	technisch	11A
temperature	ˈtempritʃə*	Temperatur	4B
temperature gauge	geidʒ	Temperaturanzeiger	5B
term	ˈtəːm	Abschnitt; Semester	10B
terminal	ˈtəːminəl	Anschluß-, Verbindungsklemme (el.)	13B
terminal block	blɔk	Lüsterklemme	11B
terribly	ˈterəbli	furchtbar	4B
test (to take a t.)		Prüfung (eine P. ablegen)	8B
test drive	draiv	Probefahrt	7B
thermometer	θəˈmɔmitə*	Thermometer	4B
thread	θred	Gewinde; Faden	2B
to think s.th. over		etwas bedenken	3A
thumb	θʌm	Daumen	1A
to be all thumbs *R*		ungeschickt sein; zwei linke Hände haben *R*	1A
to tighten	ˈtaitn	festdrehen, -ziehen (Mutter)	2B
tile	tail	Fliese; Dachziegel	1A
to tile		fliesen	1A
timber	ˈtimbə*	Bauholz	1A
time (to take t.)		Zeit brauchen	3B
in no time *R*		im Nu *R*	15A
a few times		ein paarmal	15B
timing	ˈtaimiŋ	Zündzeitpunkt	8A
tiny	ˈtaini	winzig	11B
tool	tuːl	Meißel (Maschine!)	3B
tools	tuːlz	Werkzeuge	1A
toolbox	bɔks	Werkzeugkasten	2B
tool-kit	kit	Werkzeugtasche, -kasten	11B
topped up	tɔpt	aufgefüllt	8A
torch	tɔːtʃ	Taschenlampe	11B

to touch	tʌtʃ	berühren	11B
to tow	təu	abschleppen	9A
traffic (heavy)	ˈtræfik	Verkehr (dichter V.)	78, 8B
traffic jam	dʒæm	Verkehrsstau	9A
traffic signs	sainz	Verkehrszeichen	8B
trafficator	ˈtræfikeitə*	Blinker	5B
trafficator lever	ˈliːvə*	Blinkerhebel	5B
trailer	ˈtreilə*	Anhänger	9B
to transform	trænsˈfɔːm	umspannen (el.)	14B
transformer	trænsˈfɔːmə*	Transformator	14B
transistor	trænˈsistə*	Transistor	15B
trouble	trʌbl	Ärger, Sorgen	6B
trunk (U.S.)	trʌŋk	Kofferraum	5A
trunk road	roud	Bundesstraße; Fernverkehrsstraße	9A
tube (picture t.)	tjuːb	Bildröhre	15A
tube		Schlauch	5A
tubeless	ˈtjuːblis	Schlauchlos (Reifen)	5A
to tune	tjuːn	abstimmen (Sender)	15B
tuning		Abstimmung	15B
turbine	ˈtəːbin; təːbain	Turbine	14B
to turn on – off	təːn	an-, abstellen	3B
turning tool		Drehmeißel	3B
turret lathe	ˈtʌrit leið	Revolverdrehmaschine	3B
type	taip	Typ	
tyre (tire U.S.)	taiə*	Reifen	

U

ugly	ˈʌgli	häßlich	14A
undercoat	kəut	Farbanstrich	1B
to unlock		aufschließen	4B
to unscrew		auf-, losschrauben	13B
until	ənˈtil	bis	8A
uranium	juˈreinjəm	Uran	14A
urgent	ˈəːdʒənt	dringend	13A
to use		benutzen; verbrauchen	6B, 11A
to use up		aufbrauchen	6B
used (get used to)	ˈjuːstə	sich gewöhnen an	8B
useful		nützlich	2A
usual	ˈjuːʒuəl	gewöhnlich	3A

V

valve	vælv	Ventil	5A, 10A
valve cap		Ventilkappe, -verschluß	5A
vehicle	ˈviːikl	Fahrzeug	
ventilation control lever	ˌventiˈleiʃən kənˈtrəul	Lüftungsregulierungs-hebel	5B
vents (fresh air v.)	vents	Lüftungsschlitze	5B
vernier caliper	ˈvəːniə ˈkælipə*	Schieblehre; Meß-schieber	3C
vice	vais	Schraubstock	2B
visit (to pay s.b. a. v.)	ˈvizit	jem. besuchen	1A
volt (voltage)	vɔlt; ˈvəultidʒ	Volt (el.) Spannung	12A

W

wages	ˈweidʒiz	Lohn	10B
wallpaper	ˈwɔːlpeipə*	Tapete	1A
wallsocket	ˈsɔkit	Wandsteckdose	11A
waltz	wɔːls	Walzer	15A
to warn	wɔːn	warnen	4A
warning flasher	ˈflæʃə*	Warnblinkleuchte	5B
warning lights		Kontrolleuchten	5B
washer	ˈwɔʃə*	Dichtungsring	4A
to watch out		aufpassen (Verkehr)	8B
watt	wɔt	Watt	11A
way (by the w.) *R*		übrigens *R*	2B
way (to give w.)		Vorfahrt lassen	8B
way (right of w.)		Vorfahrt	8B
ways (in different w.)		auf verschiedene Weise	3B
weak	wiːk	schwach	12A
weak current	ˈwiːk ˈkʌrənt	Schwachstrom	12A
to wear	ˈwɛə*	sich abnutzen	3C
to weld	weld	schweißen	4A
welder	ˈweldə*	Schweißer	4A
welding gear	ˈgiə*	Schweißgerät	4A
welding rod	rɔd	Schweißstab	4A
welding shop		Schweißerei	4B
welding torch	tɔːtʃ	Schweißbrenner	4A
well (as well as) *R*		sowie auch; ebenso wie *R*	8A
wet		naß	9B
what about *R*		wie steht es mit ...? was ist mit ...? wie wäre es mit ...? *R*	2B

whatever		was auch immer	1A
what's on *R*		was gibt es (TV; Radio etc.) *R*	15B
wheel	wiːl	Rad	5A
wheel spanner	ˈspænə*	Kreuzschlüssel	7B
whole (on the w.) *R*	houl	im großen und ganzen *R*	4B, 14A
to wind, wound –	waind	wickeln	13B
wing mirror	ˈwiŋ ˈmirə*	Außenrückspiegel	5A
wing nut	nʌt	Flügelmutter	2B
wing screw	skruː	Flügelschraube	2B
window handle	ˈhændl	Fensterkurbel	5B
windscreen; windshield (U.S.)	ˈwindskriːn ˈwindʃiːld	Windschutzscheibe	5A
wire	ˈwaiə	Draht; Leitung	2B, 11B, 12B
wire stripper	ˈstripə*	Abisolierzange	11B
to wonder (I wonder) *R*	ˈwʌndə*	geht es wohl, daß …? ist es möglich, daß …?	8A
		ich frage mich, ob …? *R*	8B
woodscrew	ˈwudskruː	Holzschraube	2B
woodwork		Holzarbeit, Bastelei	2B
workman	ˈwəːkmən	Facharbeiter	2A
workpiece		Werkstück	3B
workshop		Werkstatt	2A
to worry (don't w.)	ˈwʌri	sich sorgen; keine Sorgen machen	8B
wrench (monkey w.)	rentʃ-ˈmʌŋki	Schraubenschlüssel (verstellbar)	2B

X

x-ray	ˈeksˈrei	Röntgenstrahl	14A

Y

yourself (do it y.) *R*	jɔːˈself	mach es selbst *R*	1A

Deutsch – Englisch

A

Abblendlicht	dipped beam	5A
Abblendlichtschalter	dipswitch	5B
abfließen lassen (einlassen)	to release	14B
abgehen (sich losdrehen)	to come off	2B
abgesehen von	apart from	12A
Abisolierzange	insulation stripping pliers (wire stripper)	11B
ablegen (abheften)	to file	2A
ablegen (Prüfung)	to take a test	8B
abnutzen (sich a.)	to wear, wore, worn	3C
abschleppen	to tow	9A
abschmieren (Fett)	to grease	3C
abschmieren (Öl)	to lubricate	3C
Absonderung	isolation	11B
Absperrhahn	stop cock	4A
abstellen (anhalten)	to stop	3B
abstimmen (Sender)	to tune	15B
Abstimmung (Sender)	tuning	15B
abstreifen	to strip off	11B
abwürgen (Motor)	to stall	8B
abziehen (entfernen)	to remove	11B
Akte	file	2A
also; deshalb	so	9A
Ampere	ampere	12A
amtlich	official	9A
anbringen (befestigen)	to fix	3B
anbringen (installieren)	to install	4A
Anfänger	beginner	3B
Angebot (günstig; Sonder-)	bargain	1B
Anhänger	trailer	9B
anhören (sich a., klingen)	to sound	8B
anlassen (Motor, Maschine)	to start	3B, 6A
Anlasser	starter	6A
annehmen (erwarten)	to expect	13A
annehmen (vermuten)	to believe	15B
ansaugen (ziehen)	to draw	10A
Ansaughub(-takt)	induction stroke	10A
anschließen (el.)	to connect	12B
Anschluß (el.)	connection	12B

Anschlußstelle (el.)	socket outlet; power outlet	13A
Anschlußklemme	terminal	13B
ansteigen (Temperatur)	to rise	14A
an-, abstellen	to turn on, - off	3B
anspringen (Motor)	to start	6A
Anstrich	coat	1B
Antenne	aerial	5A
Anzeige (Zeitung)	advertisement	1B
Anzeigegerät	indicator	4B
anzeigen	to indicate	4B
anzeigen (Zeichen geben)	to signal	6A
Arbeits- (Montage)-Anleitung	set of instructions	1B
Arbeitskollege	fellow	14A
Arbeitsvorgang	operation	3B
Architekt	architect	11A
Ärger, Sorgen	trouble	6B
ärgerlich	annoying	12A
Armaturen (Beschläge)	fittings	13A
Armaturenbrett (Auto)	dashboard	5B
Armstütze	arm rest	5B
Art	kind of	3B
Aschenbecher	ashtray	5B
atomar	atomic	14A
Atomkraftwerk	atomic power station	14A
Atommeiler	atomic pile	14A
auch nicht	no(not) either	11A
aufbrauchen	to use up	6B
aufgefüllt	topped up	8A
aufgeregt	excited	4B
aufheizen	to heat up	14A
aufladen (Batterie)	to charge	8A
aufpassen (Verkehr)	to watch out	8B
aufpumpen	to inflate	5A
aufschließen	to unlock	4B
im Auge behalten	to keep an eye on	3C
Ausdauer	perseverance	10B
auseinanderhalten	to keep apart	9B
auseinandernehmen (Maschine)	to disassemble	3C
ausgehen (Benzin, Geld)	to run out of	6B
Auspuff; Ausstoß	exhaust	10A
Auspuffrohr	exhaust pipe	5A
Auspufftopf	silencer	5A
Ausstoßtakt	exhaust stroke	10A
Außenrückspiegel	wing mirror	5A
außer	except for	9A

außerdem auch	as well (as)	11B
das Äußere; äußerlich	exterior	5A
aussuchen	to choose	1A
Austritt, Auslaß	outlet	10A
auswechseln	to change, exchange	7B
Auto	car; motor-car	3A, 5A
Autobahn	motorway	9A
Autobahnauffahrt	access point	9B
Autobahnausfahrt	exit	9B
Autofabrik (Werksanlagen)	plant (car assembly plant)	10B
Autofahrer	motorist	8A
Autohändler	car dealer	7A
automatisch	automatic	3B
Autostraße (Bundesstraße; Fernverkehrsstraße)	trunk road	9A
Autowerkstatt	garage	3A

B

Bastelei (Holzarbeit)	woodwork	2B
Bauholz	timber	1A
Bauteil (Einzelteil; Stück)	piece	1B
bearbeiten (Material)	to process	3B
bedenken (etwas)	to think something over	3A
bedienen (Maschine)	to operate	3A
Bediener (Maschine)	operator	3A
Bedienungsanleitung	operating instruction(s)	3C
Bedienungstasten (-knöpfe)	controls	15B
befestigen	to fix	3B
befestigt an	to be attached to	11B
Beifahrersitz	passenger seat	5B
benötigen	to need	1A
benutzen	to use	11A
Benzin	petrol	9B
bergig	mountainous	14B
berühren (sich)	to touch	11B
beschädigen	to damage	11B
beschleunigen	to accelerate	5B
bessern (sich b.; verbessern)	to improve	15B
bestehen (Prüfung)	to pass	8B
besuchen	to pay somebody a visit	1A
Beton	concrete	14A
Beule (Delle)	dent	5A

Bild (ein B. vermitteln; informieren)	to put somebody in the picture	4B
Bildröhre	tube; picture tube	15B
Bildschirm	screen	15B
bis	until	8A
bißchen (ein b.)	slightly	15B
blanker Draht	bare wire	13B
bleiben bei (Sache; Grundsatz)	to stick to	14A
bleiben lassen (etwas)	to leave something	15A
Blick (auf einen B.)	at a glance	4B
Blick (auf den ersten B.)	at first glance	4B
Blinker	trafficator; traffic indicator	5A
Blinkerhebel	trafficator lever	5B
bloß (nur; eben)	just	9A, 3B
bohren	to drill; to bore	1A, 3B
Bohrer	drill	1A
Bohrer (zum Einsetzen)	bit	1A
Bohrmeißel	boring tool	3B
Bohrplattform (-insel)	drilling rig	4B
Bolzen	bolt	2B
bremsen	to brake	5B
Bremslichter	brake lights	5A
Bremspedal	brake pedal	5B
Brennkammer (-raum), Motor,	combustion chamber	10A,
Brennstäbe (Atom)	fuel rods	14A
Brett	board	1A
Broschüre	brochure	13A
Bücherschrank	bookcase	1A
Bügelsäge	frame saw	2B
Büro	office	2A
Büroangestellte(r)	clerk	2B
Bursche	chap	4B

C

Chemiewerk (Anlage)	chemical plant	4B

D

Dach	roof	5A
Dampf	steam	14A

Dampfturbine	steam turbine	14B
Daumen	thumb	1A
Deckel	lid	5A, 15A
Decker (Oberteil eines Steckers)	plug cover	13B
Defekt (Fehler)	fault	4A
deshalb	so	9A
dicht (nahe bei; nahe dran)	close	9B
Dichtungsring	washer	4A
Draht (Leitungsdraht)	wire	2B
Drehmaschine, Drehbank	lathe	3A
drehen (sich d.)	to rotate	3B
Drehknopf	knob	3B
Drehmeißel	turning tool	3B
Drehstrom	three-phase-current	12A
drin (drinnen)	inside	8A
dringend	urgent	13A
Druck	pressure	4B
drücken	to press	3B
Dübel; Mauerdübel	rawl plug	2B
durchgehen (-laufen, el.)	to pass	12B, 14B
durchgehen (Liste überprüfen etc.)	to check	2B
Durchlauferhitzer	hot water geyser	4A
durchsprechen (einen Plan, eine Sache)	to check	11A

E

ebenso wie	as well as	8A
eigentlich	as a matter of fact	3A
Eierkocher	egg boiler	11A
einfach	simple	11B
einfach (bloß; nur)	just	3B, 9A
einhaken; befestigen	to fasten	6A
einerseits – andererseits	on the one hand – on the other hand	2A
einlassen (Abwasser in einen Fluß)	to release	14B
Einlaßventil	inlet valve	10A
einleuchtend sein	to make sense	14A
einrichten	to set up; to set	2A, 3B

einschlafen	to fall asleep	9B
einsetzen	to fix	3B
einspannen (Werkstück)	to put in	3B
einstellen (regulieren)	to adjust; to set	2B
einstöpseln	to plug	13A
einweisen (in fließenden Verkehr)	to guide	6A
Einzelheiten	details	11A
Eisen	iron	2B
Eisensäge	hacksaw	2B
Eisenwarenhandlung	hardwareshop	2B
Elektriker	electrician	11A
elektrisch	electric	1A
		11A
Elektrizität	electricity	11B
Elektroherd	cooker	11A
empfehlen	to recommend	9A
Empfehlung	recommendation	9A
Energie	energy	14A
eng	narrow	9A
enthalten	to contain	14A
entladen (Batterie)	to discharge	8A
Entriegelungshebel	release	5B
entschieden (eine Sache ist e.)	to be definite	14A
Ersatzteil	spare part	3C
Erdleitung (Erdung)	earth wire	12B
erfahren (im Beruf)	experienced	3B
Erfahrung	experience	3B
Ergebnis	result	1B
erklären	to explain	4B
Erneuerung (Fahrbahndecke)	resurfacing	9A
ersetzen	to replace	3C
erstemal (das e.; zum e.)	the first time	7B
explodieren	to explode	14A
Explosion	explosion	10A
explosiv	explosive	10A
extra	special	3B
		11A
Extras (Autozubehör)	extras	7A

F

Fabrik	factory	3A
Facharbeiter	workman	2A
Fachmann	expert	2A
Fahrbahn (Autobahnseite)	carriageway	9B

Fahrbahndecke	surface	9A
fahrbereit	in running order	7A
fahren (Rad; Moped; Motorrad)	to ride	6A
fahren (Auto)	to drive	5B
Fahrersitz	driver's seat	5B
Fahrgestell	chassis	5A
Fahrprüfung	driving test	8B
Fahrspur (Autobahn)	lane	9A
Fahrt aufnehmen (Geschwindigkeit)	to gather speed	6A
Fahrzeug	vehicle	9B
falls	in case; if	9A
Farbanstrich	undercoat	1B
Faser	strand	11B
Fassung	socket	11A
Feder (im Deckel)	spring	15A
Feile	file	2A
feilen	to file	2A
Felge	rim	5A
Fensterkurbel	window handle	5B
Fernlicht	full beam	5A
Fernverkehrsstraße (Bundesstraße)	trunk road	9A
fertig	finished	8A
fest	firm (-ly)	15A
festdrehen (anziehen)	to tighten	2B
flicken	to mend	13A
Fliese	tile	1A
fliesen	to tile	1A
Fließband	assembly line	10B
fließen (el.)	to flow	12B
flimmern (TV)	to flicker	15B
Flugblatt (Beilage)	leaflet	1B
Flügelmutter	wing nut	2B
Flügelschraube	wing screw	2B
fordern	to demand	10B
formdrehen	to form turn	3B
Fortschritt	progress	14A
fräsen	to mill	3B
Fräsmaschine	milling machine	3B
Fräser (Schneidwerkzeug)	milling cutter	3B
Fuchsschwanz	handsaw	2B
Fuge	joint	1B
Führerschein	driving licence	8B
fummeln	to fumble	15A

Funken	spark	4A
Funktion	function	3B
furchtbar	terrible, -bly	4B
Fußgängerübergang	pedestrian crossing	8B

G

Gallone	gallon	7A
Garantie	guarantee	7A
Gang (erster)	bottom gear	6A
Gang (rückwärts)	reverse gear	6A
Gaspedal	accelerator pedal	5B
Gebiet (Bezirk)	district	14A
Gebläse	fan	5A
Gebrauchtwagen	second-hand car	7A
Gebrauchsanweisung	directions for use	3C
gefährlich	dangerous	6B
Gefühl (ein G. entwickeln für)	to develop an instinct	4B
Gegend	region	9B
gehen (es könnte g.)	it might do	15A
geht es wohl, daß	I wonder if	8A
Geldstrafe	fine	6B
gelegen kommen	to come in handy	13A
Gelenk	joint	1B
genau so	exactly	6B
generalüberholt (Auto)	reconditioned	7A
Generator	generator	14B
genug	enough	6B
genügend (ausreichend)	sufficient	14A
gerade	straight	1A
Gerät (el.)	electric appliance	11A
Gerät (TV, Radio)	set	15B
Gerät (fest montiert)	fixed appliance	12A
geschickt	skilful	2A
Geschirrspülautomat	dishwasher	11A
Geschwindigkeit	speed	3B, 6A
Geschwindigkeitsbegrenzung	speed limit	9A
Geschwindigkeitsüberschreitung (rasen)	speeding	6B
gesunder Verstand	common sense	8B
Getriebe	gear	10A
Getriebeautomatik	automatic transmission	5B
Gewinde	thread	2B

gewöhnen	to get used to	8B
Gewohnheit	routine	4B
Gleichstrom	direct current; d.c.	12A
Gliedermaßstab (Zollstock)	rule	1A
Glück haben	to be lucky	7B
Glückwunsch	congratulation	8B
Glühbirne	bulb	6B
gratulieren	to congratulate	8B
griffbereit	to be handy	3C
Griffe	handles	11B
Größe	size	1A
im großen und ganzen	on the whole	4B, 14A
Grundausrüstung	basic equipment	2A
grundieren	to prime	1B
Grundierung	primer	1B
Gurt	seat belt	5B
Gurtverriegelung	seat belt buckle	5B

H

Haltestreifen (-platz)	lay-by	9B
Hammer	hammer	1A
hämmern	to hammer	1A
Handbremse	handbrake	5B
Handsäge	handsaw	2B
Handschuhfach (Auto)	glove compartment	5B
Harfe	harp	3A
häufig	frequent (-ly)	9B
Hauptfließband	main line	10B
Hauptleitung (Strom, Wasser)	mains	4A
Haushaltsgeld	housekeeping money	2A
Haushaltsstrom	domestic electricity	12A
Hausmeister	caretaker	4A
Hebel	lever	3B
Hebevorrichtung (Kran)	hoist	10B
Heckscheibe	rear window	5A
Heimwerker	do it yourself enthusiast	1A
Heimwerkermarkt (Einkaufszentrum für H.)	d.i.y. center	1A
Heißwasseranlage (-versorgung)	hot water supply	4A
heizbar (beheizt)	heated	5A
Heizgerät (-lüfter)	electric heater	12A
Heizkessel	boiler	4B

Heizungsschalter	heater switch	5B
Helligkeit	brightness	15B
herumführen	to take s.b. round	4B
hineinstecken (einstöpseln)	to plug	13A
Hinweis	hint	2A, 8B
Hobel	plane	2B
hobeln (langhobeln)	to plane	2B, 3B
hochdrücken (-schieben; Hebel)	to push up	3B
hochheben (-pumpen) (Auto)	to jack up	7B
hochspannen (Strom)	to change up	14B
Hochspannungsleitung	power line	14B
Hochspannungsmast	pylon	14B
hochziehen	to hoist	10B
Holzschraube	woodscrew	2B
Hubschrauber	helicopter	9A
hügelig	hilly	9B
Hügelkuppe	brow of a hill	8B
Hupe	horn	5A
Hutmutter	cap nut	2B

I

Idee	idea	3A
im Nu	in no time	15A
Industriegesellschaft	industrial society	14B
Ingenieur	engineer	4B
Innenrückspiegel	inside rear view mirror	5B
Inneres (innen)	interior	5B
Inspektion (Auto)	service	7A
Installateur (Gas, Wasser)	plumber	2B
instinktiv	instinctively	8B
Isolation (Absonderung)	isolation	11B
Isolator	insulator	11B
Isolierband	insulating tape	11B
isolieren (el.)	to insulate	11B
isolieren (absondern von)	to isolate	11B
isoliert (el.)	insulated	11B
Isolierung (el.)	insulation	11B

J

jedenfalls (wie dem auch sei)	anyway	3A
jemals	ever	8B

K

Kabel	cable	12B
Kabel (3gliedrig)	flex; flexible cord	13B
Kabelklemme	cord grip	13B
Kabelsteckdose (Kupplung)	cable socket	13A
Kanal (TV)	channel	15B
Kanalwählschalter	channel selector	15B
Kantine	canteen	4B
kaputt gehen	to break	3C
kaputt sein	to be broken	3C
Karosserie	body	5A
Kassettenrekorder	cassette recorder	15A
kaum jemals	hardly ever	11A
Kernspaltung	nuclear fission	14A
Kessel, Tank	tank	4B
Kettenreaktion	chain reaction	14A
Kilometerzähler	odometer	5B
Kippschalter	rocker switch (tumbler switch)	13A
klein (unbedeutend)	minor	11B
Klemme	clamp	11B
Kneifzange	pincers	2B
Knopf	button	3B
Kofferraum	boot; trunk (U.S.)	5A
Kofferraumdeckel	boot lid	5A
Kohlenbergwerk	coal mine	4B
Kolben	piston	10A
Kombiwagen	estate car; station wagon (U.S.)	4A
Kombizange	pliers	2B
komisch	funny	3A
kommen lassen (Kupplung)	to release	6A
kompliziert	complicated	3C
Kontermutter	lock nut	2B
Kontrast	contrast	15B
Kontrolleuchten	warning lights	5B
Kopf (Schraube; Bolzen)	head	2B
Kopfstütze	head rest	5B
Kotflügel	mudguard, fender (U.S.)	5A
Kraftstoff (Brennstoff)	fuel	7A
Kraftstoffanzeiger (Benzinuhr)	fuel gauge	5B
Kraftwerk	power station	14A
Kreuz (über Kreuz)	crosswise	7B
Kreuzschlüssel	wheel spanner	7B
Kügelchen	pellets	14A
Kühlergrill (-gitter)	radiator grill	5A

Kühlschrank	refrigerator (fridge)	11A
Kühlturm	cooling tower	14A
Kunde	customer	7A
Kupplungspedal	clutch pedal	5B
kürzen (einschränken)	to cut down	2A
Kurzhobler	shaping machine; shaper	3B
Kurzschluß	short circuit	12B
Kurve	bend	8B

L

Lackierung	top coat	1B
Lampenstecker	lamp plug	13A
Landschaft	landscape	14A
langdrehen	straight turning	3B
länger dauern	to take longer	15A
Langhobelmaschine	planing machine (planer)	3B
langweilig	dull	10B
Lastkraftwagen	lorry	9B
laufen (normal l., rund laufen – Mot.)	to run smoothly	6A
Laubsäge	fret saw	2B
Lautsprecher	speaker	15A
Leck	leak	4A
leer (Batterie)	flat	8A
Leerlauf	neutral gear	6A
Lehrling	apprentice	4B
leicht (etwas)	slightly	15B
Leitung	wire	11B, 12B
Lenkrad	steering wheel	5B
Lenkung	steering	7A
Leuchtröhre	fluorescent light	11A
Lichthupe	hazard flasher	5B
Lichtmaschinenanzeiger	generator warning light; ignition light	5B
Lichtschalter	light switch	13A
Loch	hole	1B
Lohn	wages	10B
lose (locker)	loose	2B
lose (nicht el. angeschlossen)	stray	13B
lösen (lockern)	to loosen	2B
lösen (Bremse, Kupplung)	to release	6A

losfahren	to start off	8B
losfahren (langsam)	to move off	6A
losschrauben	to unscrew	13B
löten	to solder	4A
Löter	solderer	4A
Lötgerät	soldering gear	4A
Lötkolben	soldering iron	4A
Lüftungsregulierungshebel	ventilation control lever	5B

M

mach es selbst	do it yourself	1A
malen (streichen)	to paint	1B
markieren	to mark	1B
Markierung	mark	1B
Maschine	machine	3A
Maschinist	machinist	3B
Maßangaben (Maße)	measurements	1B
Material	material	1A
Mauerdübel	rawl plug	2B
Mechaniker	mechanic	2A
Mehrfachsteckdose (Tischsteckdose)	socket panel	13A
meinen	to mean	13A
Meißel	chisel	1A
Meißel	tool	3B
melden ([sich] m. bei)	to report to	10B
Menschenskind!	blimey	6B
Meßgerät	gauge; gage (U.S.)	4B
Metall	metal	3B
Metallfassung (-rahmen)	metalwork	12B
mindestens	at least	11A
möglich	possible	11A
möglich (ist es wohl m., daß ...)	I wonder if	8A
montieren	to fit	2B
Monteur	fitter	3C
Motor (Auto; Flugzeug)	engine	3A
Motorhaube	bonnet; hood (U.S.)	5A
Muffe	joint	4A
Mutter	nut	2B

N

Nadel	needle	4B
Nadel (Plattenspieler)	stylus	15A
Nagel	nail	1A
Nagelbohrer	gimlet	2B
nagelneu	brand new	8B
nähern (sich n.)	to approach	8B
naß	wet	9B
Nebelleuchten	fog lights	5A
Nebelschlußleuchte	rear fog light	5A
nebenan	next door	3A
Neonlicht	fluorescent light	11A
neulich	the other day	4A
nichts als, nichts außer	nothing but	6B
Nullleiter	neutral wire	12B
Nummernschild	number plate	5A
Nut (Rille)	groove	3B
nützlich	useful	2A

O

obwohl	although	15B
Ofen (Industrie; Zentralheizung)	furnace	14B
Öldruckmesser	oil pressure gauge	5B
Ölgesellschaft	oil corporation	4B
Ölstand	oil level	6A
ordentlich	properly	15A
Ordnung (in O. bringen)	to fix; to put something right	3B, 6B

P

Panne	breakdown	9A
Parkplatz	parking area (lot); car park	9B
passen	to fit	2B
Personalchef	personell manager	10B
Physiker	physicist	14A
plandrehen (stirndrehen)	to face	3B
platt (Reifen)	flat	8A
Plattenspieler	record player	15A
Pleuelstange	con rod (connecting r.)	10A

praktisch	practical	8B
Presse	press	3B
pressen	to press	3B
Preßluftschraubenschlüssel	power wrench	10B
Produktion	production	14A
produzieren	to produce	14A
Profil	profile	3B
Prüfung ablegen	to take a test (examination)	8B
Punkt (nächster P.)	next item	2B
Punktschweißen	spot welding	10B

Q

Quittung	receipt	8A

R

Rad	wheel	5A
Radio	radio	5B
Radioaktivität	radioactivity	14A
Radkappe	hub cap	5A
Rasenmäher	lawn mower	2B
Rat; Ratschlag	advice	2A
rausspringen (Sicherung)	to blow	12A
reagieren	to react	8B, 14A
Reaktion	reaction	14A
Reaktor	reactor	14A
Rechnung	bill	2A
Regal (Regalbrett)	shelf	1A
Regel	rule	13A
regelmäßig	regular(ly)	3C
regeln (regulieren)	to regulate	3B
Regierung	government	14A
Reifen	tyre; tire (U.S.)	5A
Reifenpanne	puncture	7B
reindrücken	to push in	3B
renovieren	to renovate	11A
reparieren	to repair	1A
Reparatur (-tätigkeit)	repair job	1A
Reserverad	spare wheel	7B
Revolverdrehmaschine	turret lathe	3B
Richtung	direction	9B
riesig	gigantic	14A

Röntgenstrahlen	x-rays	14A
Rohr	pipe	4A
Rohrleitung (Fernleitung)	pipeline	4B
Rohrleitungsanlage	pipe system	4B
Rückblickspiegel	rear view mirror	5A
Rückfahrscheinwerfer	reversing lights	5A
Rückleuchten	rear lights	5A
Rundstahl	round bar steel	3B

S

sachte (sanft)	gently	6A
Säge	saw	1A
sägen	to saw; to cut	1A
Satz (Werkzeuge)	set	1A
Sauerstoff-Azetylenzylinder	oxy acetylene cylinder	4A
schalten (Auto, rauf-, runter)	to change up, - down	6A
Schalter	switch	3B
Schalthebel (Auto)	gear lever	5B
schätzen	to appreciate	15A
Scharniere	hinges	2B
Scheibenwischer	windscreen wiper	5A
Scheinwerfer (Auto)	headlights	5A
Schicht (Arbeit)	shift	10B
Schieblehre (Meßschieber)	vernier caliper	3C
schlag (-stoß)gesichert (el.)	shockproof	13A
Schlauch	tube	5A
schlauchlos	tubeless	5A
schließen	to close	10A
schließen (vervollständigen)	to complete	12A
schließlich (letzten Endes)	after all	14A
schließlich	in the end	4A
Schloß	[1]) lock; [2]) door lock; [3]) boot lock	4B, 5A
Schlosser	locksmith	4B
schmal	narrow	9A
Schmieröl	lubricant	3C
schneiden (auf Maß)	to cut to size	1B
Schornstein	chimney	14A
Schraubenschlüssel	spanner	2B
Schraubenschlüssel (verstellbar)	wrench	2B
Schraubenzieher	screwdriver	1A
Schraubstock	vice	2B
schrecklich	dreadful	9B

Schritt halten mit	to keep up with	10B
Schukostecker	shrouded contact plug	12B
Schutzbrille	safety goggles	4A
schützen vor	to protect from	4A
Schutzhelm	helmet	4A
Schutzkleidung	protective clothing	4A
Schuppen	shed	2A
schwach	weak	12A
Schwachstrom	weak (low voltage) current	12A
Schweißbrenner	welding torch	4A
schweißen	to weld	4A
Schweißer	welder	4A
Schweißerei	welding shop	4A
Schweißgerät	welding gear	4A
Schweißschirm	handshield	4A
Schweißstab	welding rod	4A
schwer, steif (Lenkung d. Autos)	stiff	7A
schwierig	difficult	8B
sechseckig	hexagonal	2B
Seitenstreifen (Autobahn)	hard shoulder	9A
Semester	term	10B
Sicherung	fuse	6B
Sicherungsdraht erneuern	to rewire a fuse	12A
Sicherungskasten	fuse box	12A
sichtbar	exposed	12B
Skala	scale	4B
Skizze	sketch	14A
Sorgen (sich keine S. machen)	don't worry	8B
sowie auch	as well as	8A
sowieso	anyway	3A
sozusagen	as it were	14A
Spannung	voltage (volt)	12A
Spannung verringern	to step down	14B
sparen	to save	2A
Spiel haben (Lenkung)	a bit slack	7A
Spielverderber	spoilsport	2B
Spitzenverkehrszeit	rush hour	8B
Stahlplatte	steel plate	4A
Stahlwerk	steel plant	4B
Stand (Niveau)	level	6A
Standlicht	parking light	5A
Standspur	hard shoulder	9A
Stanze	punching machine	3B
stanzen, lochen	to punch	3B
Starkstrom	power current	12A

Starterklappe	manual choke	5B
statistische Angaben	statistics	8B
Stecker, Stöpsel	plug	12A
Stellknopf	adjusting knob	5B
Steuerungsanlage	control system	4B
stirnfräsen	shell-end-milling	3B
stoßen (hobeln)	to shape	3B
Stoßstange	bumper	5A
strahlen (Licht)	to glare	4A
strahlen	to radiate	14A
Strahlung	radiation	14A
Straßenbauarbeiten	roadworks	9A
Straßenkreuzung	road junction	8B
Straßenverkehrsordnung	highway code	8B
Streifenwagen	patrol car	9A
Strom (el.)	electric current; power	12A
Stromanschlußstelle	power outlet	13A
stromführende Leitung	live wire	12B
Stromkreis	circuit (current circuit)	11A
Stromquelle	source of power	12B
Stromverbrauch	consumption of current	12A

T

Tachometer	speedometer	5B
Tankklappe (-verschluß)	petrol cap	5A
Tankstelle	service station; filling station (U.S.)	3A
Tankstellenwärter	attendant	8A
Tapete	wallpaper	1A
tapezieren	to paper	1A
Taschenlampe	torch	11B
technisch	technical	11A
Temperatur	temperature	4B
Temperaturanzeiger	temperature gauge	5B
Tempo (Schritt, Bewegung)	pace	10B
teuer	expensive	9A
Thermometer	thermometer	4B
Tiefkühltruhe	deepfreezer	11A
Tip	hint	2A, 8B
Tischsteckdose	socket panel	13A
Ton	sound	15B
Tonband	tape	15A

Tonbandgerät	(tape) recorder	15A
Transformator	transformer	14B
Transistor	transistor	15B
Treibstoff	fuel	7A
treten (durchtreten, Kupplung, Gas)	to depress	6A
Turbine	turbine	14B
Türgriff	door handle	5A
Typ	type	1A

U

überhaupt nicht (keine Ursache)	not at all	8A
überholen	to overtake	6A
überladen (-lasten, el.)	to overload	11A
überlassen	to leave	3C
übernachten	to stay the night	9B
überrascht sein	to be surprised	2A
überschreiten (Geschwindigkeit)	to exceed	9A
Überzug	covering (sheathing)	13B
übrigens	by the way	2B
Uhrzeigersinn (im U.)	clockwise	6A
Ufer	bank	14A
Umdrehung	revolution	3B
Umhüllung (Schutzschicht)	sheathing	11B
umspannen (el.)	to transform	14B
Umspannwerk	sub station	14B
unbesonnen (leichtfertig)	reckless	8B
Unfall	accident	8B
ungeschickt sein	to be all thumbs	1A
unter, unterhalb	below	14A
unter, (darunter)	beneath	14B
unterbrechen (el.)	to break	12A
Unterbrecherkontakte	contact breaker points	8A
Unterlegscheibe	spacer	2B
unterschiedlich	different	1A
unvermeidlich	inevitable	14A
Uran	uranium	14A
Ursache	cause	9B

V

Ventil	valve	5A, 10A

Ventilator	fan	5B
Ventilkappe	valve cap	5A
verantwortlich sein	to be responsible	4B
verarbeiten	to process	3B
verbinden (el.)	to connect	12B
Verbindungsstelle (-stück)	joint	1B
Verbrauch	consumption	7A
verbrauchen	to consume	7A
Verbrennungsmotor	combustion engine	10A
verderben	to spoil	14A
Verdichtung	compression	10A
Vergaser	carburettor	8A
Verkehr	traffic	7A
Verkehr (dicht)	heavy traffic	8B
Verkehrsstau	traffic jam	9A
Verkehrszeichen	traffic signs	8B
Verlängerungskabel	extension flex	13A
Verlängerungsschnur	extension lead	13A
verlassen (sich verl. auf)	to rely on	4B
verlieren	to lose	2B
Vermittlung (Tel.)	operator	3A
vermuten	to suppose	6B
verschiedene	several	2B
Verschlußmutter	stop nut	2B
verschmutzen	to pollute	14B
Verschmutzung	pollution	14B
verrückt sein	to be nuts	2B
versprechen	to promise	3A
Verteilerdose	distribution box	11A
Verteilerkopf	distributor head	10A
verwirrend	confusing	9A
verzögern	to retard	14A
viereckig; Viereck	square	2B
Viertaktmotor	four stroke engine	10A
Viertel	quarter	6B
völlig	absolutely	6B
vollständig	complete	13A
Volt	voltage, volt	12A
Vorarbeiter	foreman	4B
Vorfahrt lassen	to give way	8B
Vorfahrtsrecht	right of way	8B
vorgefertigt	prefabricated	1B
Vorschlag	suggestion	11A
vorschlagen	to suggest	2A, 11A

vorsichtig	cautious(-ly)	8B
vorstellen (sich etwas v.)	to imagine	15A
vorziehen	to prefer	11B
vorzugsweise	preferably	11B

W

Waagerechtstoßmaschine (Kurzhobler)	shaping machine, shaper	3B
Wagenheber	car jack	7B
Wahl (keine W. haben)	to have no choice	14A
Walzenfräser (Meißel)	plain milling cutter	3B
Walzer	waltz	15A
walzfräsen	to slab-mill	3B
Wandsteckdose	wall socket	11A
Warnblinkleuchte	warning flasher	5B
warnen	to warn	4A
warten (pflegen)	to service	7A
Wartung (Auto)	maintenance	7A
was auch immer	whatever	1A
was gibt's (Programm TV, Radio)	what's on	15B
was ist mit (wie steht's mit; wie wäre es mit)	what about	2B
Wasserhahn	tap	4A
Wasserkraftwerk	hydro electric power station	14B
Watt	watt	11A
Wechselstrom	alternating current a.c.	12A
weich	soft	4A
Weise (auf verschiedene W.)	in different ways	3B
Werkbank	(work)-bench	2A
Werkstück	piece of material; workpiece	3B
Werkzeuge	tools	1A
Werkzeugkasten	tool box	2B
Werkzeugtasche (-kasten)	tool kit	11B
wichtig	important	4B
wickeln	to wind, wound	13B
Windschutzscheibe	windscreen	5A
winzig	tiny	11B

Z

Zeit (eine Frage der Z.)	a matter of time	8B
Zeit brauchen	to take time; it takes time	3B

Zeitabstand	interval	3C
Zentralheizung	central heating	4A
Ziegel	tile	1A
ziehen (ansaugen)	to draw	10A
Zimmerdecke	ceiling	11A
Zubehör	accessories	13A
zu bleiben	to stay closed	15A
Zufall	accident	8B
Zugschalter	pull-cord switch	13A
Zukunftsaussichten	prospects	4B
Zulassungsnummer	licence number	5A
zünden	to ignite	10A
Zündschloß	ignition switch	5B
Zündschlüssel	ignition key	5B
Zündspule	coil	10A
Zündzeitpunkt	timing (– of ignition)	8A
zurechtkommen mit	to cope with	11B
zurückschalten (Auto)	to change down	6A
zurücksetzen (Auto)	to reverse	6A
zusammendrücken	to compress	10A
zusammenfügen	to join together	1B
zusammensetzen (Maschine etc.)	to assemble	3C
zusammensetzen (wieder z.)	to reassemble	3C
zusätzlich	additional	13A
zuschließen	to lock	4B
zustimmen	to agree with	11A
zylindrisch	cylindrical	3B

Listen

Tools (metal) – Werkzeuge (Metall)

anvil	[ˈænvil]	Amboß
ball-pane hammer	[pein]	Ausbeulhammer
blow torch	[tɔːtʃ]	Lötgebläse
bolt clipper	[bəult ˈklipə*]	Bolzenschneider
cable shears	[keibl ʃiəz]	Kabelschere (-zange)
chipping hammer	[ˈtʃipiŋ]	Meißelhammer (Schweißarbeit)
combination pliers	[kɔmbiˈneiʃən ˈplaiəz]	Kombizange
conduit bending pincers	[ˈkɔndit ˈbendiŋ ˈpinsəz]	Rohrdrahtbiegezange (el.)
eyelet pliers	[ˈailit]	Ösenzange
file (flat file)	[flæt fail]	Feile
flat-nose pliers	[flæt nouz]	Flachzange
hacksaw	[ˈhæksɔː]	Eisensäge
insulation stripping pliers (wire stripper)	[ˌinsjuˈleiʃən] [ˈstripiŋ; ˈstripə*]	Abisolierzange
lead-tin (solder)	[led-tin; sɔːldə*]	Lötzinn
pincers		Kneifzange
pipe wrench (adjustable)	[rentʃ; əˈdʒʌstəbl]	Rohrzange (verstellbar)
plate shears	[pleit ʃiəz]	Blechschere
ring spanner		Ringschlüssel
rivet set	[ˈrivit]	Nietenzieher
riveting hammer		Niethammer
round file	[fail]	Rundfeile
round-nose pliers		Rundbiegezange
rubber mallet	[ˈrʌbə ˈmælit]	Gummihammer
screwdriver	[ˈskruːˌdraivə*]	Schraubenzieher (-dreher)
socket wrench	[ˈsɔkit]	Steckschlüssel
soldering torch	[ˈsɔːldəriŋ ˌtɔːtʃ]	Lötlampe
spanner	[ˈspænə*]	Schraubenschlüssel
sparking plug spanner	[ˈspɑːkiŋ ˌplʌg]	Zündkerzenschlüssel
square	[skwɛə]	Winkel
thread cutting stock	[ˈθred ˈkʌtiŋ stɔk]	Gewindeschneidkluppe
vernier caliper	[ˈvəːniə ˈkælipə*]	Schieblehre (Meßschieber)
vice	[vais]	Schraubstock

welding rod	[ˈweldiŋ rɔd]	Schweißstab
welding torch		Schweißbrenner
wire brush	[ˈwaiə brʌʃ]	Drahtbürste
wrench (monkey wrench)	[ˈmʌŋki]	Schraubenschlüssel (verstellbar)

Werkzeuge (Metall) – Tools (Metal)

Abisolierzange	insulation stripping pliers; wire stripper
Amboß	anvil
Ausbeulhammer	ball-pane hammer
Blechschere	plate shears
Bolzenschneider	bolt clipper
Drahtbürste	wire brush
Eisensäge	hacksaw
Feile	file; flat file
Flachzange	flat-nose pliers
Gewindeschneidkluppe	thread cutting stock
Gummihammer	rubber mallet
Kabelschere (-zange)	cable shears
Kneifzange	pincers
Kombizange	combination pliers
Lötgebläse	blow torch
Lötlampe	soldering torch
Lötzinn	lead-tin solder
Meißelhammer (Schweißarbeit)	chipping hammer
Nietenzieher	rivet set
Niethammer	riveting hammer
Ösenzange	eyelet pliers
Ringschlüssel	ring spanner
Rohrdrahtbiegezange (el.)	conduit bending pincers
Rohrzange (verstellbar)	pipe wrench (adjustable)
Rundbiegezange	round-nose pliers
Rundfeile	round file
Schieblehre (Meßschieber)	vernier caliper
Schraubenschlüssel	spanner
Schraubenschlüssel (verstellbar)	wrench (monkey wrench)
Schraubenzieher	screwdriver
Schraubstock	vice
Schweißbrenner	welding torch
Schweißstab	welding rod
Steckschlüssel	socket wrench
Winkel	square
Zündkerzenschlüssel	sparking plug spanner

Tools and material for woodwork and manual work
Werkzeuge und Material für Holz- und Bastelarbeit

adhesive	[əd'hi:ziv]	Klebstoff
adhesive tape	[teip]	Klebeband, -streifen
bits	[bits]	Bohreinsatz für Hand- und el. Bohrer
brace	[breis]	Bohrer (Handbohrer)
cardboard	['kɑ:dbɔ:d]	Pappe
circular saw	['sə:kjulə sɔ:]	Kreissäge
chisel	['tʃizl]	Meißel
compass saw	['kʌmpəs sɔ:]	Lochsäge (Stichsäge)
corrugated cardboard	['kɔrugeitid]	Wellpappe
drawing pin	['drɔ:iŋ .pin]	Reißbrettstift (Heftzwecke)
drill chuck	[tʃʌk]	Bohrerhalter -Futter
electric drill	[i'lektrik]	Bohrer (el.)
folding rule	['fəuldiŋ ru:l]	Zollstock, Gliedermaßstab
frame saw	[freim sɔ:]	Bügelsäge
fret saw	[fret]	Laubsäge
gimlet	[gimlit]	Nagelbohrer
glass paper; sand paper	[glɑ:s; sænd 'peipə*]	Schmirgelpapier
glue	[glu:]	Leim
hand saw		Handsäge (Fuchsschwanz)
hard wood fibre board	['faibə bɔ:d]	Preßholzplatte (Hartfaser), Spanplatte
(chipboard)	['tʃipbɔ:d]	
mallet	['mælit]	Holzhammer (schlegel)
nail (galvanized)	[neil; 'gælvənaizd]	Nagel (verzinkt)
pair of compasses	['pεər əv 'kʌmpəsiz]	Zirkel
pincers	['pinsəs]	Zange (Kneifzange)
plane	[plein]	Hobel
plastics	['plæstiks]	Kunststoff
plywood	['plaiwud]	Sperrholz
rasp	[rɑ:sp]	Raspel
saw		Säge
sawblade	['sɔ:bleid]	Sägeblatt
screw clamp; cramp	[skru: klæmp; kræmp]	Zwinge

scissors	[ˈsizəz]	Schere
spirit level	[ˈspirit ˈlevəl]	Wasserwage
tape measure	[ˈteip ˈmeʒə]	Bandmaß
varnish	[ˈvɑːniʃ]	Lack; Firnis

Werkzeuge und Material für Holz- und Bastelarbeit
Tools and material for woodwork and manual work

Bandmaß	tape measure
Bohrer (Handbohrer)	brace
Bohrer (el.)	electric drill
Bohreinsatz für Hand- und el. Bohrer (Pl.)	bits
Bohrerhalter	drill chuck
Bügelsäge	frame saw
Handsäge (Fuchsschwanz)	hand saw
Hobel	plane
Holzhammer (Schlegel)	mallet
Klebeband (-streifen)	adhesive tape
Klebstoff	adhesive
Kreissäge	circular saw
Kunststoff	plastics
Lack (Firnis)	varnish
Laubsäge	fret saw
Leim	glue
Lochsäge (Stichsäge)	compass saw
Meißel	chisel
Nagel (verzinkt)	nail (galvanized)
Nagelbohrer	gimlet
Pappe	cardboard
Preßholzplatte (Hartfaser, Spanplatte)	hard wood fibre board, chipboard
Raspel	rasp
Reißbrettstift (Heftzwecke)	drawing pin
Säge	saw
Sägeblatt	saw blade
Schere	scissors
Schmirgelpapier	glass paper; sandpaper
Sperrholz	plywood
Wasserwaage	spirit level
Wellpappe	corrugated cardboard

Zange	pincers
Zirkel	pair of compasses
Zollstock, Gliedermaßstab	folding rule
Zwinge	screw clamp; cramp

Metals and alloys – Metalle und Legierungen

alloy	[ˈælɔi]	Legierung
aluminium	[ˌæljuˈminjəm]	Aluminium
brass	[brɑːs]	Messing
bronze	[brɔnz]	Bronze
cast brass	[kɑːst]	Messingguß
cast iron	[ˈaiən]	Gußeisen
cast steel	[stiːl]	Gußstahl
copper	[ˈkɔpə*]	Kupfer
copper coat	[kəut]	Kupferüberzug
copper coated	[ˈkəutid]	verkupfert
corrugated sheet steel	[ˈkɔrugeitid ʃiːt stiːl]	Wellblech
foil (thin sheet)	[fɔil]	Folie
galvanized	[ˈgælvənaizd]	verzinkt
galvanized sheet		Zinkblech
gold	[gəuld]	Gold
heavy metal	[ˈhevi ˈmetl]	Schwermetall
heavy sheet plate	[pleit]	Grobblech
iron; iron ore	[ˈaiən ɔː*]	Eisen; Eisenerz
lead	[led]	Blei
light metal	[lait metl]	Leichtmetall
light sheet		Feinblech
nickel	[ˈnikl]	Nickel
nickel coated, nickel plated	[ˈkoutid] [pleitid]	vernickelt
sheet metal		Bleche (allg.)
silver	[ˈsilvə*]	Silber
steel		Stahl
tempered steel	[ˈtempəd]	vergüteter Stahl
tin	[tin]	Zinn
tin metal sheet		Zinnblech
zinc	[ziŋk]	Zink

Metalle und Legierungen – Metals and alloys

Aluminium	aluminium
Bleche (allg.)	sheet metal
Blei	lead
Bronze	bronze
Eisen; Eisenerz	iron, iron ore
Feinblech	light sheet
Folie	foil (thin sheet)
Gold	gold
Grobblech	heavy sheet plate
Gußeisen	cast iron
Gußstahl	cast steel
Kupfer	copper
Kupferüberzug	copper coat
Legierung	alloy
Leichtmetall	light metal
Messing	brass
Messingguß	cast brass
Nickel	nickel
Silber	silver
Schwermetall	heavy metal
Stahl	steel
vergüteter Stahl	tempered steel
verkupfert	copper coated
vernickelt	nickel coated, nickel plated
verzinkt	galvanized
Wellblech	corrugated sheet steel
Zink	zinc
Zinkblech	glavanized sheet
Zinn	tin
Zinnblech	tin metal sheet

Building material and other materials
Baumaterial und andere Werkstoffe

brick	[brik]	Ziegel
hollow brick	[ˈhɔləu]	Hohlbaustein (Hohlziegel)
tile	[tail]	Dachziegel
glass brick	[glɑːs brik]	Glasbaustein
facing brick	[ˈfeisiŋ]	Verblendstein

limestone	['laimstəun]	Kalkstein
sandstone	['sændstəun]	Sandstein
lime	[laim]	Kalk
sand	[sænd]	Sand
cement	[si'mənt]	Zement
concrete	['kɔŋkri:t]	Beton
lightweight concrete	['laitweit]	Leichtbeton
heavy concrete	['hevi]	Schwerbeton
coarse gravel	[kɔ:s 'grævəl]	grobkörniger Kies
fine gravel	[fain]	Feinkies
stone chipping	['tʃipiŋ]	Splitt
crushed stone	[krʌʃt]	Schotter
tar	[tɑ:*]	Teer
engineering steel	[.endʒi'niəriŋ]	Baustahl
steel fabric	[sti:l 'fæbrik]	Baustahlgewebe
reinforced concrete, ferro-concrete	[.ri:in'fɔ:st] [.ferou'kɔŋkri:t]	Stahlbeton
ferro-concrete construction	[kənstrʌkʃən]	Stahlbetonbau
to reinforce	[.ri:in'fɔ:s]	armieren, verstärken
lintel	['lintl]	Sturz (Fenster; Tür)
reinforced concrete lintel		Stahlbetonsturz
timber	['timbə*]	Bauholz
board	[bɔ:d]	Brett
plank	[plæŋk]	Bohle
log	[lɔg]	Rundholz; Stamm
girder	['gə:də*]	Träger
beam	[bi:m]	Balken
hard wood fibre board (chipboard)	[hɑ:d wud 'faibə bɔ:d] ['tʃipbɔ:d]	Hartfaserplatte (Preßholz, Spanplatte)
plywood	['plaiwud]	Sperrholz
veneer	[və'niə*]	Furnier
veneer panel	['pænl]	Furnierplatte
plaster board	['plɑ:stə bɔ:d]	Gipskartonplatte (Rigips)
insulating plate (slab)	[.insju'leitiŋ pleit] [slæb]	Dämmplatte
corrugated sheet	[kɔru'geitid]	Welleternit
tar-board	[tɑ: bɔ:d]	Teerpappe
pane of glass	[pein əv glɑ:s]	Glasscheibe
safety glass	['seifti]	Sicherheitsglas
reinforced (armoured) glass	['ɑ:məd]	verstärktes Glas
plastics (hard; soft)	['plæstiks] [hɑ:d; sɔft]	Kunststoff, (hart, weich)
plastic foams	[foum]	Schaumstoff
foam rubber	['rʌbə*]	Schaumgummi
elastic putty	[i'læstik 'pʌti]	elastischer Kitt

Baumaterial und andere Werkstoffe
Building material and other materials

Baustein (Ziegel)	brick
Hohlbaustein (Hohlziegel)	hollow brick
Dachziegel	tile
Glasbaustein	glass brick
Verblendstein	facing brick
Kalkstein	limestone
Sandstein	sandstone
Kalk	lime
Sand	sand
Zement	cement
Beton	concrete
Leichtbeton	lightweight concrete
Schwerbeton	heavy concrete
grobkörniger Kies	coarse gravel
Feinkies	fine gravel
Splitt	stone chipping
Schotter	crushed stone
Teer	tar
Baustahl	engineering steel
Baustahlgewebe	steel fabric
Stahlbeton	reinforced concrete; ferro-concrete
Stahlbetonbau	ferro-concrete construction
armieren, verstärken	to reinforce
Sturz (Fenster; Tür)	lintel
Stahlbetonsturz	reinforced concrete
Bauholz	timber
Brett	board
Bohle	plank
Rundholz (Stamm)	log
Träger	girder
Balken	beam
Hartfaserplatte (Preßholz)	hard wood fibre board
Sperrholz	plywood
Furnier	veneer
Furnierplatte	veneer panel
Gipskarton(Rigips)platte	plaster board
Dämmplatte	insulating plate (slab)
Welleternit	corrugated sheet

Teerpappe	tar-board
Glasscheibe	pane of glass
Sicherheitsglas	safety glass
verstärktes Glas	reinforced (armoured) glass
Kunststoff (hart, weich)	plastics (hard; soft)
Schaumstoff	plastic foams
Schaumgummi	foam rubber
elastischer Kitt	elastic putty

Technical jobs – crafts
Technische Berufe – Handwerksberufe

attendant; garageman (U.S.)	[.əˈtendənt] [ˈgærɑːʒmən]	Tankwart
blacksmith	[ˈblæksmiθ]	Schmied
blaster (road; quarry)	[ˈblɑːstə*; roud; ˈkwɔri]	Sprengmeister (Straßenbau; Steinbruch)
blast-furnaceman	[.blɑːst ˈfɔːnismən]	Hüttenarbeiter (Hochofen)
blower	[bləuə*]	Schmelzer (an einer Schmelzbirne)
bricklayer	[ˈbrikleiə*]	Maurer
car mechanic	[kɑː məˈkænik]	Kraftfahrzeugschlosser
carpenter	[ˈkɑːpintə*]	Zimmermann (Schreiner)
chemical engineer	[ˈkemikl .endʒiˈniə*]	Chemiker
civil engineer	[ˈsivil]	Bauingenieur
concretor	[kɔŋˈkriːtə*]	Betonierer (Betonarbeiter)
crane operator	[krein ˈɔpəreitə*]	Kranführer
draftsman, designer	[ˈdrɑːftsmən; diˈzainə]	technischer Zeichner; Konstrukteur
driller (road, quarry)	[ˈdrilə*]	Bohrer, Straßenbau, Steinbruch
driver	[ˈdraivə*]	Kraftfahrer; Fernfahrer
drop forger	[drɔp ˈfɔːdʒə*]	Gesenkschmied
electrician	[ilekˈtriʃən]	Elektriker; E.-Installateur
engine (locomotive) driver; engineer (U.S.)	[ˈendʒin] [.endʒiˈniə*]	Lokführer
fireman; stoker (U.S.)	[ˈfaiəmən; stəukə*]	Heizer
fitter	[ˈfitə*]	Monteur (Maschinenschlosser)

form setter	[fɔːm ˈsetə*]	Einschaler (Betonbau)
foundryman	[ˈfaundrimən]	Gießereiarbeiter
heating installation engineer	[ˈhiːtiŋ ˌinstəˈleiʃən]	Heizungsbauer
joiner	[ˈdʒɔinə*]	Tischler
labourer (unskilled workman)	[ˈleibərə*] [ˈʌnˈskild ˈwəːkmən]	Bauarbeiter; Bauhilfsarbeiter
locksmith	[lɔːksmiθ]	Schlosser
mason	[ˈmeisn]	Steinmetz
melter	[ˈmeltə*]	Schmelzer
milling machine operator	[ˈmiliŋ məˈʃiːn]	Fräser
miner	[ˈmainə*]	Bergarbeiter
moulder (foundry)	[mouldə*]	Former (in einer Gießerei)
physicist	[ˈfizisist]	Physiker
plasterer	[ˈplɑːstərə*]	Putzer (Bau)
plumber	[ˈplʌmə*]	Installateur (Gas; Wasser)
printer	[ˈprintə*]	Drucker
programmer	[ˈprəugræmə*]	Programmierer
radio engineer	[ˈreidiəu]	Rundfunktechniker
road builder	[roud ˈbildə*]	Straßenbauer
rolling mill engineer	[ˈrouliŋ mil]	Walzwerker
roof tiler	[ruːf ˈtailə*]	Dachdecker (Ziegel)
saw mill worker	[sɔː mil wəːkə*]	Sägewerksarbeiter
setter (machine; tool)	[ˈsetə*]	Einrichter (Maschine; Werkzeug)
slater	[ˈsleitə*]	Dachdecker (Schiefer)
storekeeper	[ˈstɔːkiːpə*]	Lagerverwalter
tiler (wall, floor)	[ˈtailə*]	Fliesenleger
toolmaker	[ˈtuːlmeikə*]	Werkzeugmacher; Werkzeugschlosser
turner (wood turner)	[ˈtəːnə]	Dreher
TV engineer	[ˈtiːˈviː ˌendʒiˈniə*]	Fernsehtechniker
welder	[ˈweldə*]	Schweißer
wood-pattern maker	[ˈpætən]	Modellschreiner

Technische Berufe – Handwerksberufe
Technical jobs – crafts

Bauarbeiter (Bauhilfsarbeiter)	labourer (unskilled workman)
Bauingenieur	civil enginer
Bergarbeiter	miner

Bergbauingenieur	mining engineer
Betonierer (-arbeiter)	concretor
Bohrer (Straßenbau; Steinbruch)	driller (road building; quarry)
Chemiker (Facharbeiter; Ingenieur)	chemical engineer
Dachdecker (Ziegel)	roof tiler
Dachdecker (Schiefer)	slater
Dreher	turner (wood turner)
Drucker	printer
Einrichter (Maschinen; Werkzeug)	setter (machine s.; tool s.)
Einschaler (Betonbau)	form setter
Elektriker (E.-Installateur)	electrician
Fernsehtechniker	TV engineer
Fliesenleger	tiler (wall t.; floor t.)
Former (in einer Gießerei)	moulder (foundry)
Fräser	milling machine operator
Gesenkschmied	drop forger
Gießereiarbeiter	foundryman
Heizer	fireman; stoker (U.S.)
Heizungsbauer	heating installation engineer
Hüttenarbeiter (Hochofen)	blast-furnaceman
Installateur (Gas; Wasser)	plumber
Kraftfahrer (Fernfahrer)	driver
Kraftfahrzeugschlosser	car mechanic
Kranführer	crane operator
Lagerverwalter	storekeeper
Lokführer	engine (locomotive) driver; engineer (U.S.)
Maurer	bricklayer
Modellschreiner	wood-pattern maker
Monteur (Masch.-Schlosser)	fitter
Physiker	physicist
Programmierer	programmer
Putzer (Bau)	plasterer
Rundfunktechniker	radio engineer
Sägewerksarbeiter	saw mill worker; sawyer (U.S.)
Schlosser	locksmith
Schmelzer	melter
Schmelzer (an einer S.-Birne)	blower
Schmied	blacksmith
Schweißer	welder
Sprengmeister (Straßenbau; Steinbruch)	blaster (road building)
Steinmetz	mason
Straßenbauer	road builder
Tankwart	attendant; garageman (U.S.)
technischer Zeichner (Konstrukteur)	draftsman; designer

Tischler	joiner
Walzwerker	rolling mill engineer
Werkzeugschlosser (-macher)	toolmaker
Zimmermann (Schreiner)	carpenter

Jobs – metalwork and woodwork
Tätigkeiten – Metall- und Holzverarbeitung

to alloy	[əˈlɔi]	legieren
to bore	[bɔː*]	maschinell bohren
to braze	[breiz]	hart löten
braze-welding	[breiz ˈweldiŋ]	schweißlöten
to cast	[kɑːst]	gießen (Eisen)
to cut		schneiden; absägen
to draw		ziehen
to drill	[dril]	bohren
to face		stirndrehen (Drehmaschine)
to file	[fail]	feilen
to forge	[fɔːdʒ]	schmieden
to form turn	[fəːm təːn]	Profil drehen (Drehmaschine)
to glue	[gluː]	leimen
to grind	[graind]	schleifen
to harden	[ˈhaːdn]	härten
to melt	[melt]	schmelzen
to mill	[mil]	fräsen
to mould	[mould]	formen (Gießerei)
to paste	[peist]	kleben
to pinch off	[pintʃ ɔf]	abknipsen, abkneifen
to plane	[plein]	hobeln (langhobeln, maschinell)
to polish	[ˈpɔliʃ]	glätten, polieren
to pour	[pɔː*]	gießen
to press	[pres]	pressen
to punch	[pʌntʃ]	stanzen, ausstanzen
to rasp	[rɑːsp]	raspeln, aufrauhen
to roll	[roul]	walzen
to rivet	[ˈrivit]	nieten
to sand	[sænd]	schmirgeln, abschleifen
to saw		sägen
to shape	[ʃeip]	stoßen, kurzhobeln (maschinell)

shell end mill	[ʃel end mil]	stirnfräsen
to slab mill	[slæb]	walzfräsen
to solder	[ˈsɔːldə*]	weich löten
to stick		kleben; ankleben
to turn		drehen (Drehbank)
to turn straight	[streit]	langdrehen (Drehmaschine)
to weld	[weld]	schweißen

Tätigkeiten – Metall- und Holzbearbeitung
Jobs – metalwork and woodwork

abknipsen, abkneifen	to pinch off
bohren	to drill; to bore (maschinell)
drehen	to turn (Drehbank); to turn straight (langdrehen); to face (stirndrehen) Drehmaschine to form turn (Profil drehen)
formen (Gießerei)	to mould
fräsen	to mill; to slab mill (walzfräsen) to shell – end mill (stirnfräsen)
feilen	to file
gießen	to pour, to cast (Eisen)
glätten	to polish
härten	to harden
hobeln	to plane; to plane (langhobeln); to shape (stoßen, kurzhobeln)
kleben (ankleben)	to stick; to paste
legieren	to alloy
leimen	to glue
löten	to solder (weich löten); to braze (hart löten); braze-welding (schweißlöten)
nieten	to rivet
pressen	to press
raspeln (aufrauhen)	to rasp
sägen (absägen)	to saw; to cut off
schmelzen	to melt
schmieden (Fabrik)	to forge
schleifen	to grind
schmirgeln (abschleifen)	to sand
schneiden	to cut

schweißen	to weld
stanzen (ausstanzen)	to punch
walzen	to roll
ziehen	to draw

Parts of Machines – Maschinenteile

general names	[ˈdʒenərəl]	*allgemeine Bezeichnungen*
movable parts	[ˈmuːvəbl pɑːts]	bewegliche Teile
frame	[freim]	Rahmen
saddle	[ˈsædl]	Werkzeugschlitten
chuck	[tʃʌk]	Spannfutter
faceplate	[ˈfeispleit]	Planscheibe
pivoted (tumbler) lever	[ˈpivətid; ˈtʌmblə* liːvə*]	Schwenkhebel
protective hood	[prəˈtektiv hud]	Schutzhaube
protective switch	[switʃ]	Schutzschalter
guard	[gɑːd]	Schutzblech
driving elements	[ˈdraiviŋ ˈelimənts]	*Antrieb*
belt	[belt]	Riemen
V-belt	[ˈviː belt]	Keilriemen
motor (electric motor)	[məutə*; iˈlektrik]	Elektromotor
emergency cut out	[iˈməːdʒənsi]	Notausschalter
limit switch	[ˈlimit switʃ]	Endschalter
gear	[giə*]	*Getriebe*
ball bearing	[ˌbɔːl ˈbɛəriŋ]	Kugellager
bearing		Lager
bevel gear	[ˈbevəl]	Kegelrad
bevelled	[ˈbevəld]	abgeschrägt
bevel pinion	[ˈpinjən]	Antriebskegelrad
cam	[kæm]	Nocken
camshaft	[ˈkæmʃɑːft]	Nockenwelle
cardan shaft	[ˈkɑːdən]	Kardanwelle
cog wheel	[ˈkɔg wiːl]	Kammrad (Zahnrad)
crankcase	[ˈkræŋkeis]	Kurbelgehäuse
crankshaft	[ˈkræŋkʃɑːft]	Kurbelwelle
drive shaft	[draiv]	Antriebswelle
driving wheel	[ˈdraiviŋ wiːl]	Antriebsrad
feed rod	[fiːd rɔd]	Zugspindel
flywheel	[ˈflaiwiːl]	Schwungrad
gear rack	[ˈgiə* ræk]	Zahnstange

gear rim	[rim]	Zahnkranz
gear wheel		Zahnrad
helical gear; spiral gear (U.S.)	[ˈhelikl] [ˈspaiərəl]	Schrägzahnrad
leadscrew	[ˈli:dskru:]	Leitspindel
roller bearing	[ˈroulə ˈbɛəriŋ]	Rollenlager
speed regulator	[spi:d ˈregjuleitə*]	Drehzahlregler
variable speed transmission	[ˈvɛəriəbl] [trænzˈmiʃən]	Stufengetriebe
worm wheel drive	[wɔ:m wi:l draiv]	Schneckenradgetriebe

Maschinenteile – Parts of Machines

Allgemeine Bezeichnungen	*general names*
bewegliche Teile	movable parts
Rahmen	frame
Schwenkhebel	pivoted (tumbler) lever
Schutzschalter	protective switch
Schutzhaube	protection hood
Schutzblech	guard
Werkzeugschlitten	saddle
Spannfutter	chuck
Planscheibe	faceplate
Antrieb	*driving elements*
Riemen	belt
Keilriemen	V belt
Endschalter	limit switch
Notausschalter	emergency cut out
Elektromotor	motor (electric motor)
Getriebe	*gear*
Antriebsrad	driving wheel
Antriebswelle	drive shaft
Antriebskegelrad	bevel pinion
abgeschrägt	bevelled
Kardanwelle	cardan shaft
Kegelrad	bevel gear
Kammrad (Zahnrad)	cog wheel
Lager	bearing
Kugellager	ball bearing
Rollenlager	roller bearing
Kurbellager	crankshaft
Kurbelgehäuse	crankcase
Nocken	cam

Nockenwelle	camshaft
Schneckenradantrieb	worm wheel drive
Schrägzahnrad	helical gear; spiral gear (U.S.)
Schwungrad	flywheel
Drehzahlregler	speed regulator
Leitspindel	leadscrew
Zugspindel	feed rod
Stufengetriebe	variable speed transmission
Zahnrad	gear wheel
Zahnkranz	gear rim
Zahnstange	gear rack

Radio and TV – General and specific terms Radio und Fernsehen – Allgemeine und spezielle Bezeichnungen

amplifier	'æmplifaiə*	Verstärker
to amplify	'æmplifai	verstärken
battery-powered	'bætəri 'pauəd	mit Batterie betrieben
built-in aerial	'ɛəriəl	eingebaute Antenne
ferrit rod aerial	'ferit ˌrɔd	Ferrit-Stab Antenne
frequency modulation	'fri:kwənsi ˌmɔdju'leiʃən	Frequenz-Modulation
high fidelity (hifi)	hai:fai'deliti–'hai'fai	höchste Klanggenauigkeit
hertz	hə:ts	Hertz, Schwingungseinheit
impedance	impi:'dəns	Wellenwiderstand
megahertz	'megəhə:ts	Megahertz
ohm	oum	Ohm, Widerstandseinheit
portable	'pɔ:təbl	tragbar
reception	ri'sepʃən	Empfang (Sendung)
reproduction	ˌri:prə'dʌkʃən	Wiedergabe (Ton, Bild)
set (radio, TV)		Gerät
speaker (loud-)		Lautsprecher
stereo	'steriou	Stereo
to tune		abstimmen, Sender einstellen
tuner	'tju:nə*	Radioteil der Phonokompaktanlage
UHF (ultra high frequency)	'ʌltrə	Ultra-Hochfrequenz = 300–3 000 Megahertz – sec.

VHF (very high frequency)		VHF = dt. UKW = 30–300 Megahertz - sec.
voltage	ˈvəultidʒ	Spannung in Volt
watt	wɔt	Watt
waveband (long, medium, short)	ˈweivbænd ˈmiːdiəm	Wellenband-Bereich Lang-Mittel-Kurz

Measures, Weights – General terms
Maße, Gewichte – Allgemeine Bezeichnungen

angle	ˈæŋgl	Winkel
area	ˈɛəriə	Fläche
capacity	kəˈpæsiti	Inhalt (Hohlmaß)
centigrade	ˈsentigreid	Grad (Thermometerskala)
circumference	səˈkʌmfərəns	Umfang
degree	diˈgriː	Grad (Winkel; Temperatur)
depth	depθ	Tiefe
diameter	daiˈæmitə*	Durchmesser
height	hait	Höhe
length	leŋθ	Länge
specific gravity	spiˈsifik ˈgræviti	spezifisches Gewicht
volume	ˈvɔljum	Inhalt (Raummaß)
weight	weit	Gewicht
width	widθ	Breite; Tiefe (Raum)

inch (in)	intʃ		= 2,540 Zentimeter
foot (ft)	fut	= 12 inches	= 30,480 Zentimeter
yard (yd)	jɑːd	= 3 feet	= 0,9144 Meter
mile (mi)	mail	= 1760 yards	= 1,609 Kilometer
(millimeter)	ˈmilimiːtə	= 0,03937 inch	= 1 Millimeter
gill (gi)	dʒil		= 142,066 Kubikzentimeter
pint (pt)	paint	= 4 gills	= 568,26 Kubikzentimeter
quart (qt)	kwɔːt	= 2 pints	= 1,136 Liter
gallon (gal)	ˈgælən	= 4 quarts	= 4,545 Liter
dram (dr)	dræm		= 1,771 Gramm
ounce (oz)	auns	= 16 drams	= 28,349 Gramm
pound (lb)	paund	= 16 ounces	= 0,453 Kilogramm
hundredweight (cwt)	ˈhʌndrədweit	= 112 pounds	= 50,802 Kilogramm (U.K.)
ton (t; tn)	tʌn	= 20 hundredweight	= 1016 Kilogramm (U.K.)